MW01629508

All Across the Spectrum

EILEEN LAMB

THOUGHT CATALOG Books

THOUGHTCATALOG.COM
NEW YORK · LOS ANGELES

Dedication

To Charlie and Jude:

You may not always find acceptance, tolerance, or compassion.

The world may not always be fair.

But I will forever be here to remind you.
That you are loved.
That you are special.
That you matter.

Be brave. Be unique. Be you.

All Across the Spectrum

France. 1996. I was six years old, standing still in front of the class, wondering why my classmates were laughing at me. I was humiliated but didn't quite understand their reaction.

That day, when the teacher asked us to sing our favorite song for the class, I chose a French song from 1935 called "Madame La Marquise," a song by a popular French singer that depicts the dialogue between a lady and her gentleman, James, who comedically downplays the death of her favorite horse. I found the song hilarious. I sang it using a deep voice to play James and a little squeaky voice for the lady. As it turned out, I was the only one who found this funny. Kids laughed, but not from joy from a prodigious performance nor because they liked the song. They were making fun of me. Sure, my song choice may have been a bit odd, and the French can be notoriously rigid, but it was the first time I looked around at my peers and thought, "Am I different?"

Growing up in France, for as long as I could remember I'd felt different from the other kids. We had different interests and when I spoke, kids often looked confused, as if I were from another planet. My love for classical music and really old songs didn't help in that regard.

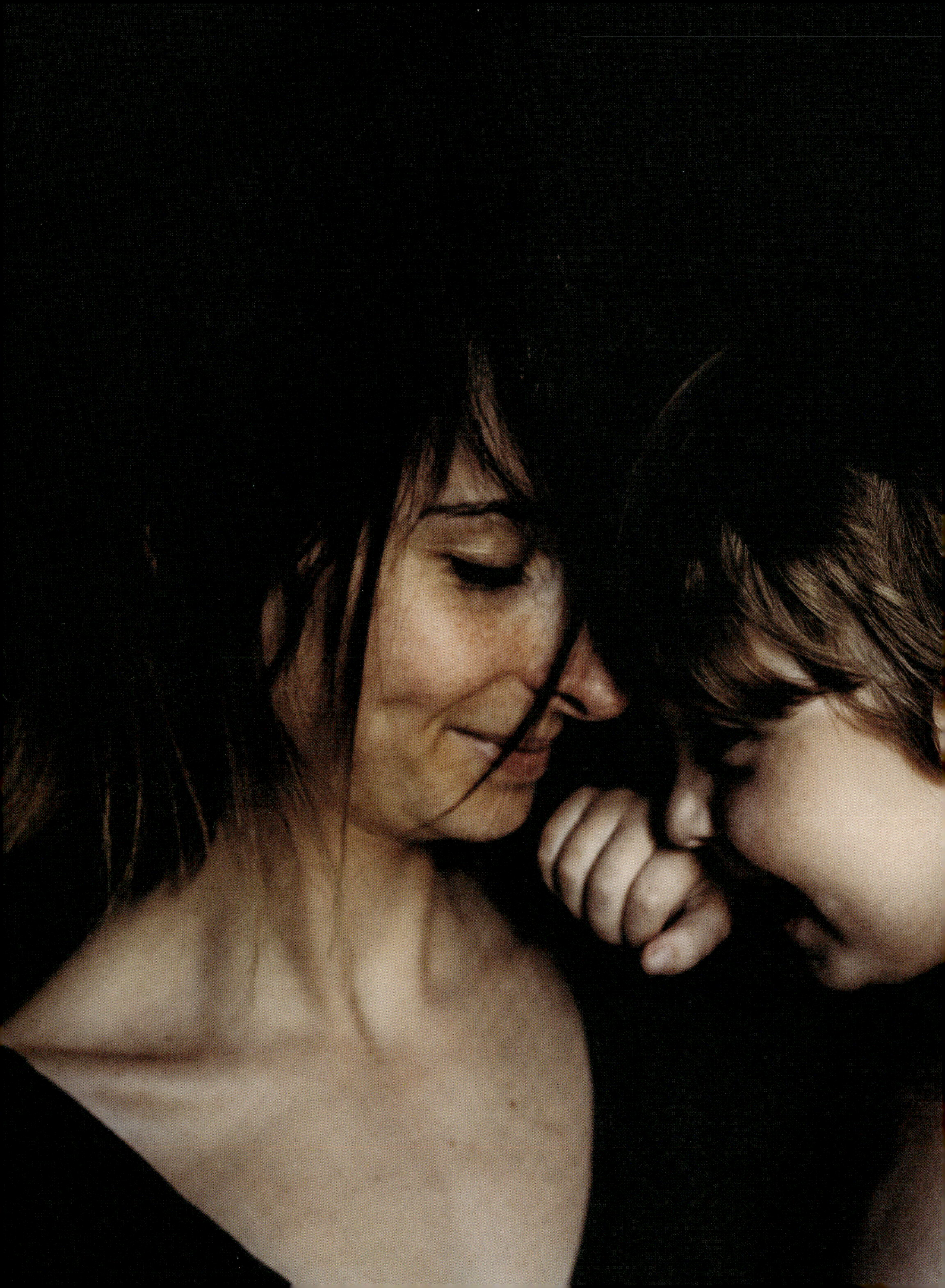

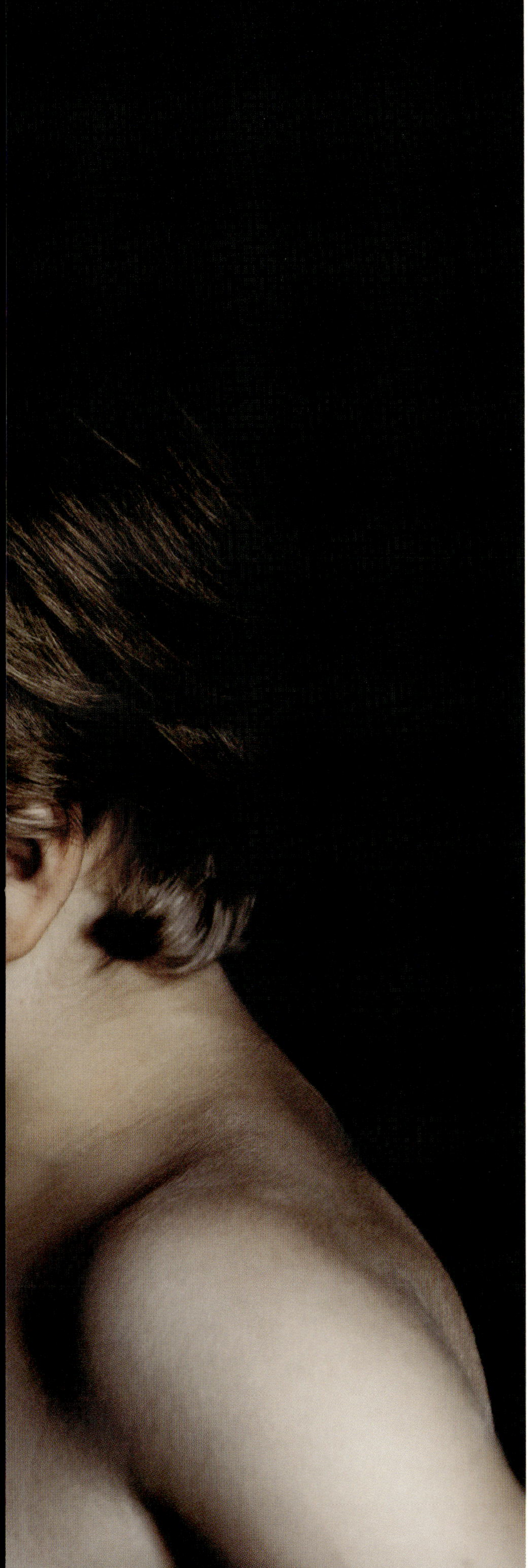

I battled through my whole life feeling out of place, just getting by. As an adult, things weren't coming any easier to me. And then I witnessed my son experiencing the same difficulties. Charlie, it turns out, has severe classic nonverbal autism and a short time after his diagnosis, I finally understood why my experiences felt so near to Charlie's. I'm autistic, too.

While Charlie and I share similar struggles, his are much more severe than mine.

Charlie is 6. At an age where his peers are learning to read and write, he still hasn't learned to talk. As times goes by, the gap between him and the other children grows and grows. As a mom, it breaks my heart to see my little boy struggle so much, struggling to do things that so many take for granted like talking or using the bathroom.

Raising a severely autistic child doesn't come with a manual—it's a constant learning experience. We go through periods of joy and pride, but there's also heartbreak and a nagging feeling of powerlessness. There's no interacting with the little human I created, there's no running to me when I come home, there's no hugging him without being pushed away. But there are many piercing screams throughout the day, screams that are constant reminders that I don't have the ability to make my son feel better. He doesn't have a way to communicate the cause of his angst. I am powerless over my child's well-being, and that is agonizing.

Being autistic and raising a severely autistic child gives me a unique perspective on the subject of autism. I see both sides of the spectrum every day: I personally live with the struggle of a disability that's often ignored because it's not obvious, and I'm fighting each day to take care of my child whose differences are extreme and apparent. Each day brings both the heartbreak of seeing my child not being able to communicate beyond very basic needs and the pure joy of a small gain like him saying "tuh" to request some toast.

I've been sharing snippets of our life for a few years now on my blog, The Autism Cafe, and I've learned along the way that there are many autistic adults out there who do not share my views on autism. They believe that only autistic individuals should be able to speak about autism because they are the ones living with it. I've also seen them countless times shame parents who express any morsel of negativity about their child's diagnosis, calling them "martyr parents." I want parents of autistic children to know that not all autistic adults share these sentiments. I don't.

I wrote this book with the hope of providing the general public with a tool to better understand the many facets of autism. I want to help parents and loved ones of people affected by autism to not feel so alone in their journey. I want to challenge stereotypes and the incessant policing of how to talk about autism that occurs through social media.

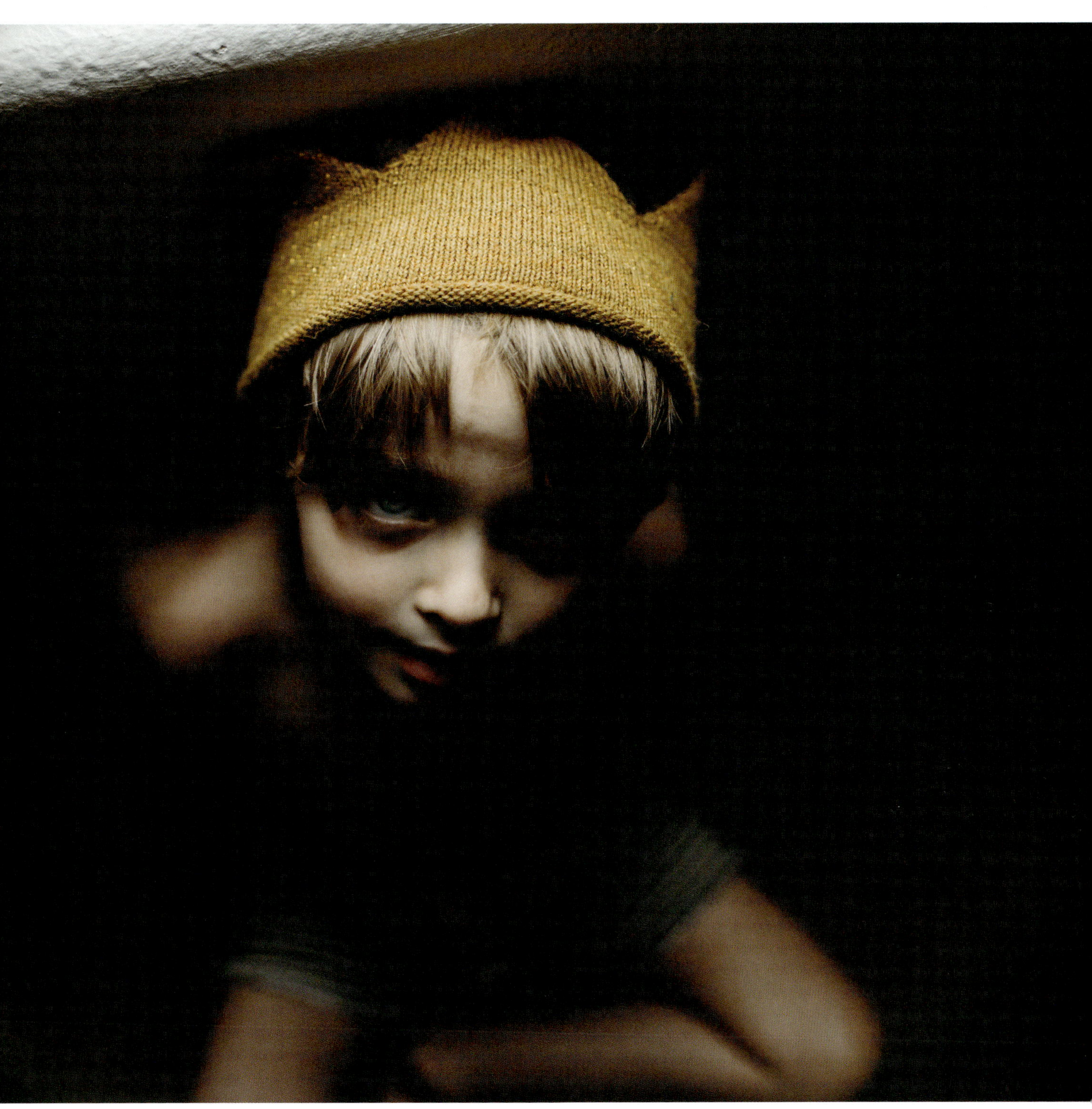

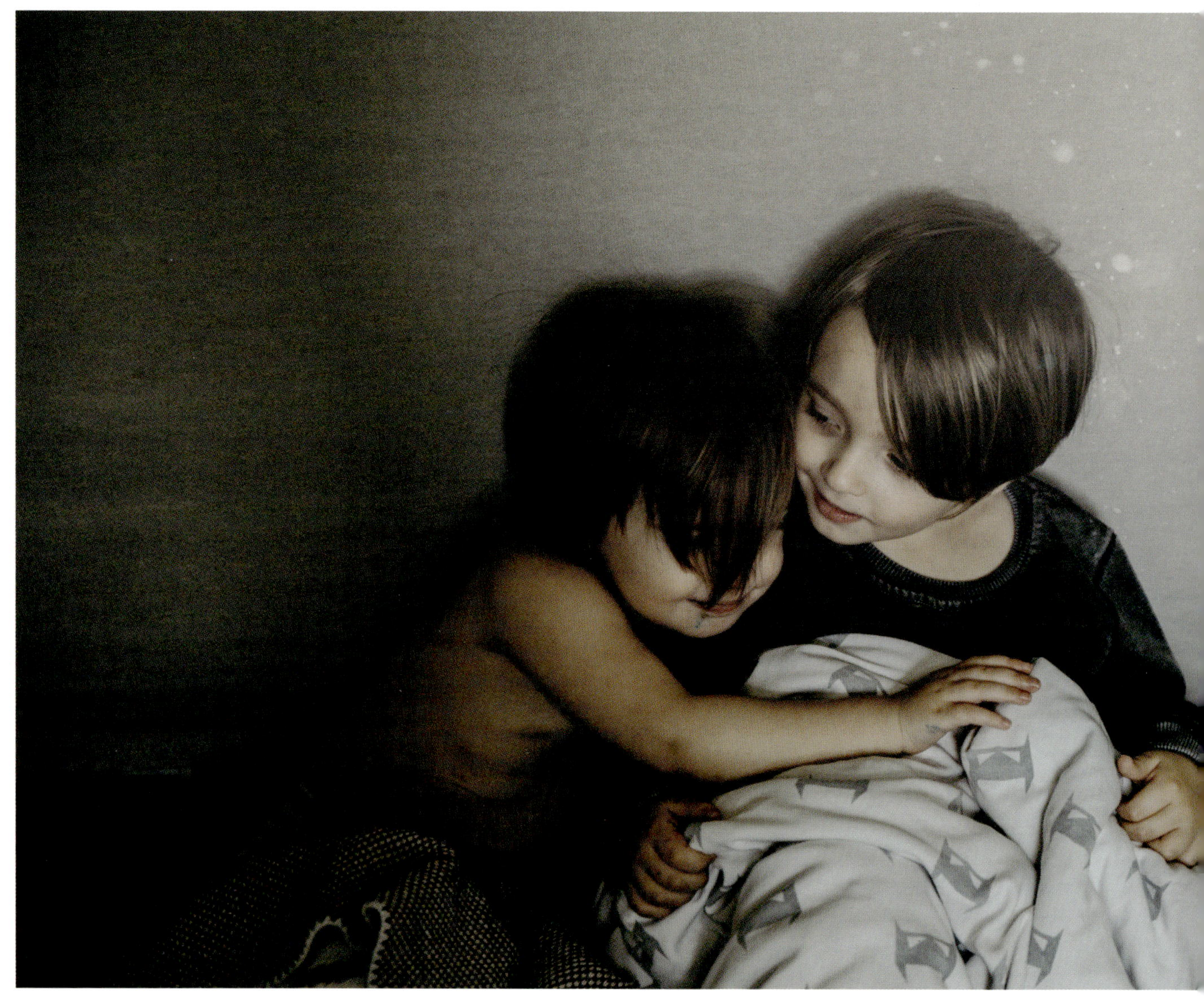

Being a parent is hard enough on its own, but raising a severely disabled child comes with its own set of struggles—we do not need the constant judgment from strangers.

We are doing the best we can to help our children and deal with our own feelings. And occasionally there are moments when we're not doing the best we can. And that's okay. But I promise you, when we fail, we're the first to be disappointed in ourselves.

In this book, I weave through stories about grieving, controversies in the autism world, growing up with an undiagnosed disability, living with an invisible disability, and also parenting an autistic child. While many people are quick to critique me for sharing my struggles as the mother of a severely autistic child, I know that there are many more parents who find comfort in my words. This book is for them. For us. I hope you find relief in knowing that there are a lot of us out there on this lonely journey.

We are not alone. You are not alone.

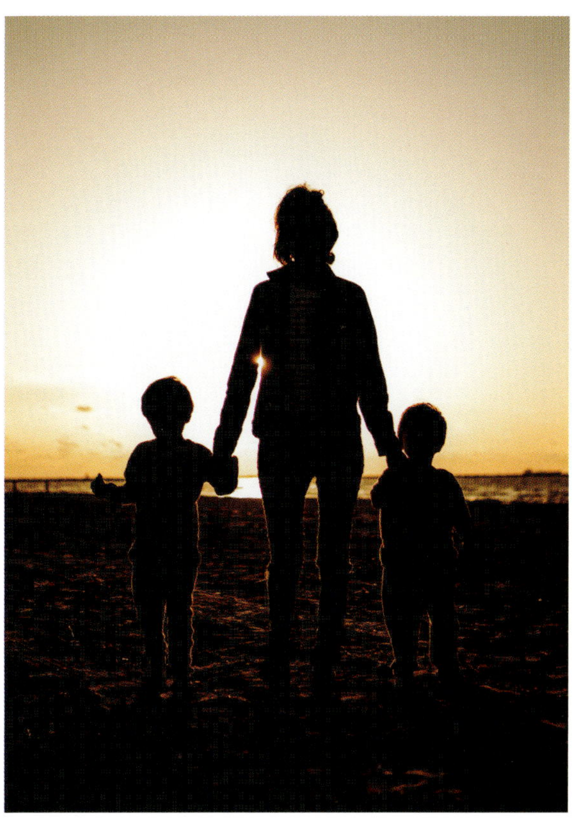

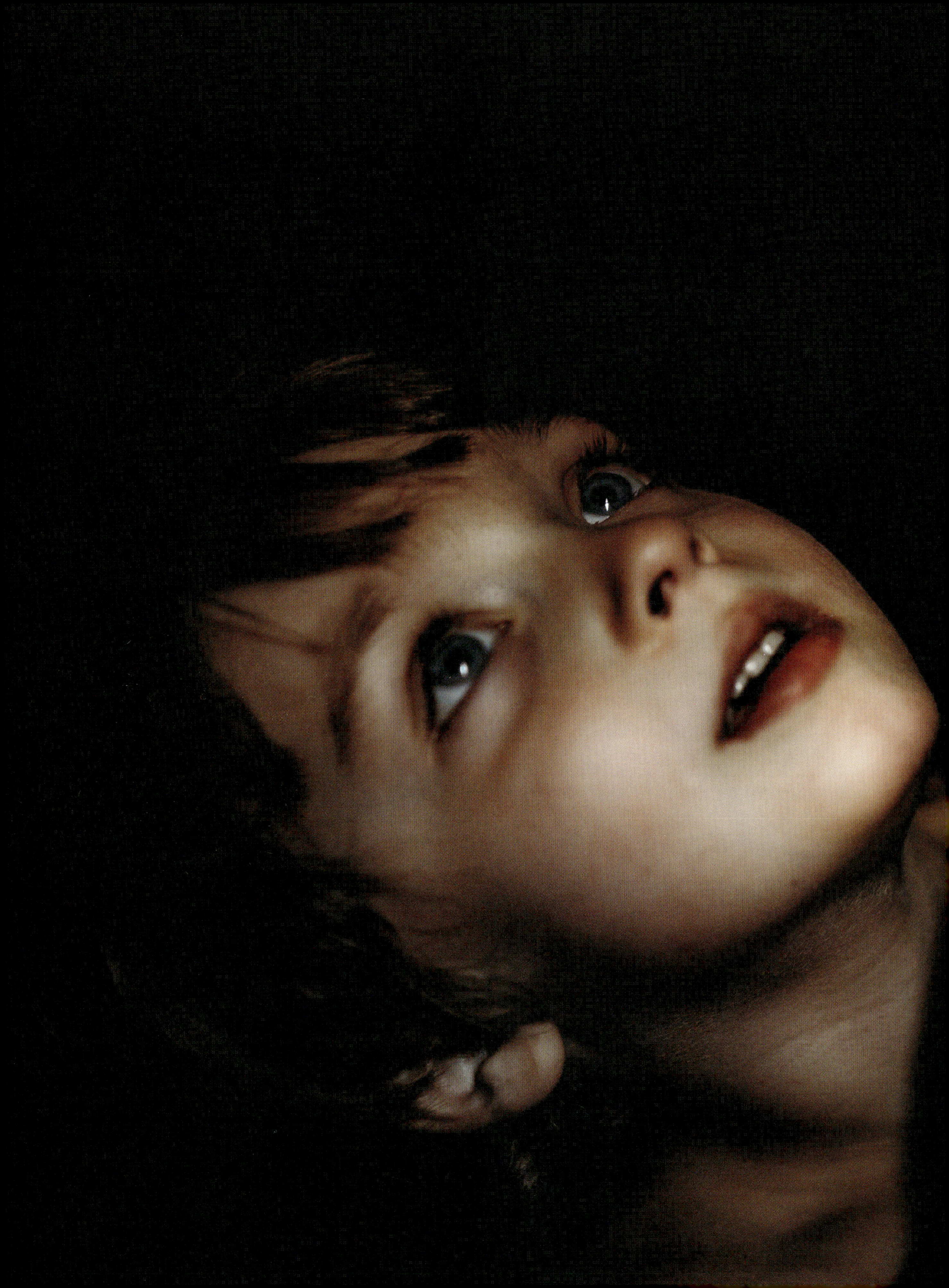

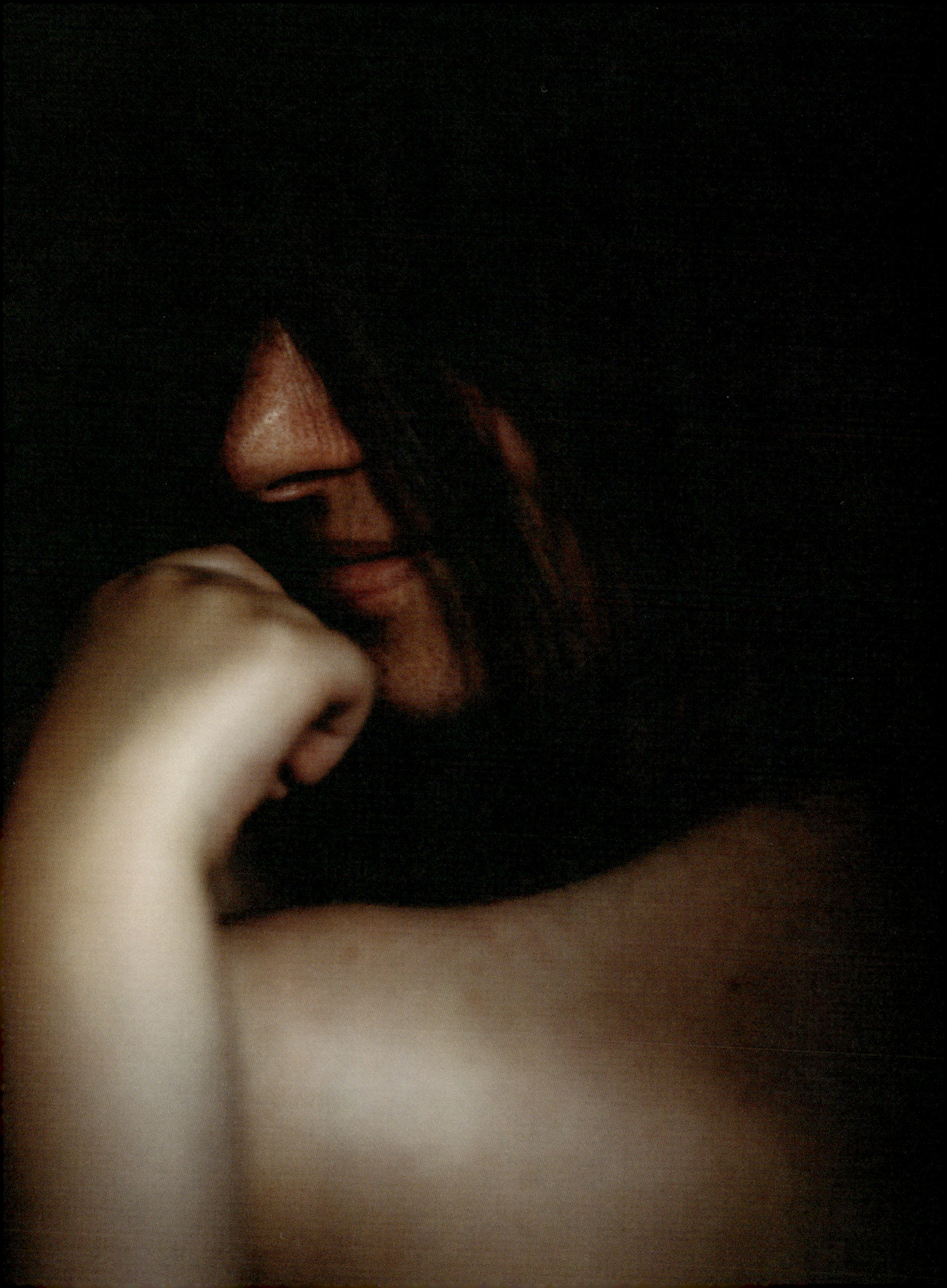

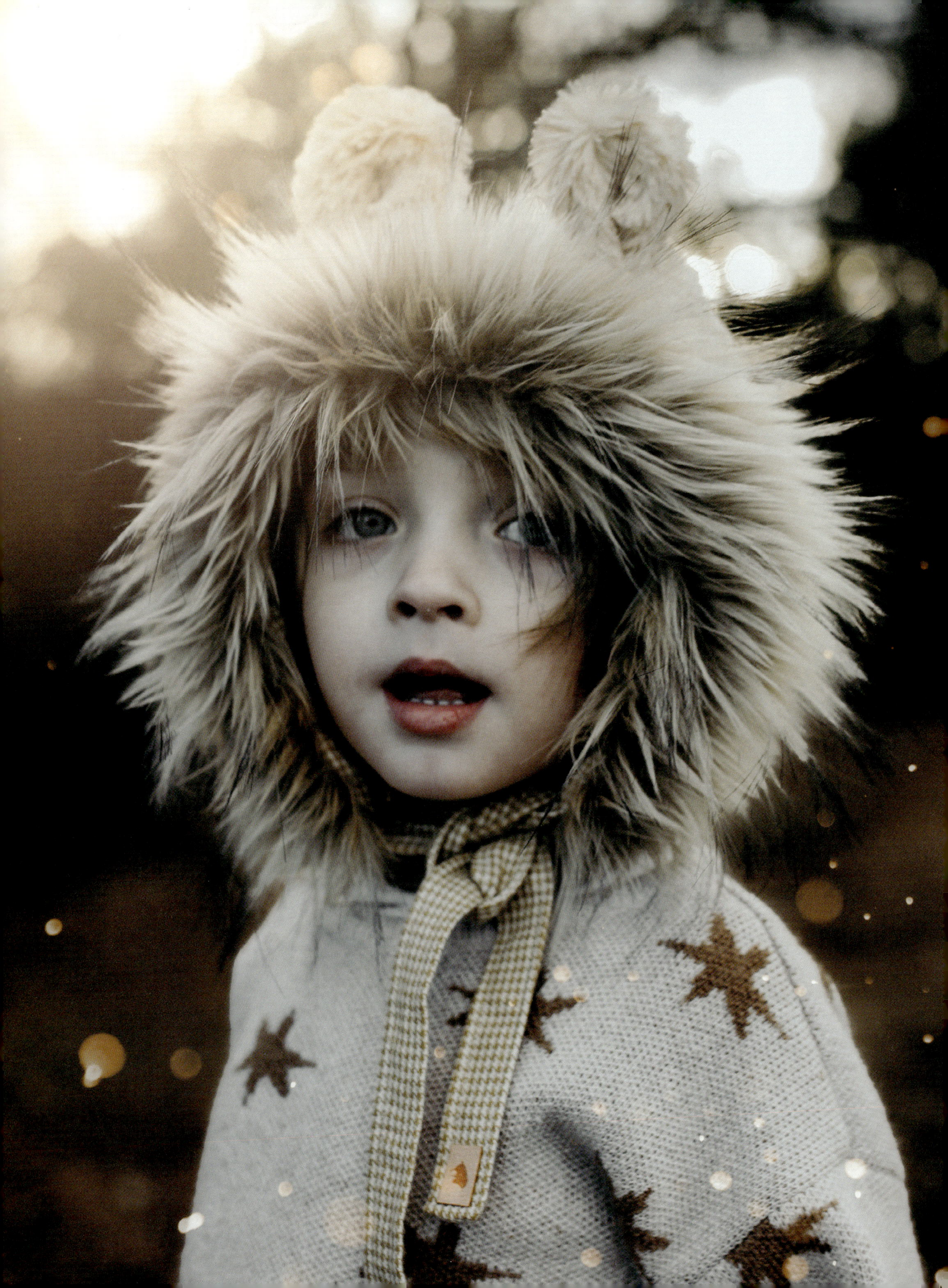

❚ Charlie? Charlie! CHARLIE! ❚

Charlie is 16 months old. Getting him to look at us when we are calling his name is, well, it's difficult. We're thinking that there's just so much to explore when you're a baby, why would he bother answering to his name when he's perfectly happy spinning a single wheel on his toy car? Now he's placing the cars in a row. Green car, red car, blue car. Charlie is such a beautiful child. He has a head as round as a pumpkin, plump rosy cheeks, and long curly blond hair that comes down well past his ears.

When Charlie's focused on a toy, he sticks his tongue out to show his extreme concentration. We don't see his big blue eyes very often, though. I used to think about how impressive it was to see him occupy himself for hours with the same toy. What a fine attention span! I appreciated his ability to block people out, appearing peaceful, like a protective bubble was insulating him from the big, new, scary world around him. Here he is, sitting on the floor with his little cars, lifting them one by one, looking at their wheels and replacing them in a perfect line. He is content.

Charlie is my firstborn, the boy I'd dreamt of having. On the day we went in for my gender-reveal ultrasound, I'd secretly kept repeating to myself, "please be a boy, please be a boy." As a child, I'd had such trouble staying friends with girls that it was clear to me I didn't understand them. They scared me. Boys, I understood better. When the ultrasound tech finally revealed that Charlie was a boy, I relaxed with the most enormous sigh of relief. A surge of happiness spread over my entire body. I would not only be his mother; he and I were going to be best friends.

Charlie was born full-term. He was the most gorgeous newborn baby I'd ever seen. I remember wondering if all parents think their baby is the most beautiful one of all, but it didn't really matter to me. He was just perfect. Although not entirely. After just a few minutes of having Charlie on my chest, something caught my eye. He had two thumbs on his right hand. There was a little extra thumb branching off of his baby thumb and the two thumbs together formed the shape of a "Y." I called my husband Willy over and showed him, and he went to find the doctor. The doctor apologized for missing the eleventh finger in his post-birth exam and assured our worried minds that things like that are not a sign of anything more serious, that the thumb could be removed surgically sometime in the future.

The months went by and Charlie was a happy baby. He was very independent, and he smiled and laughed. He especially thought it hilarious when I spoke to him in French. These little moments were like little nuggets of gold.

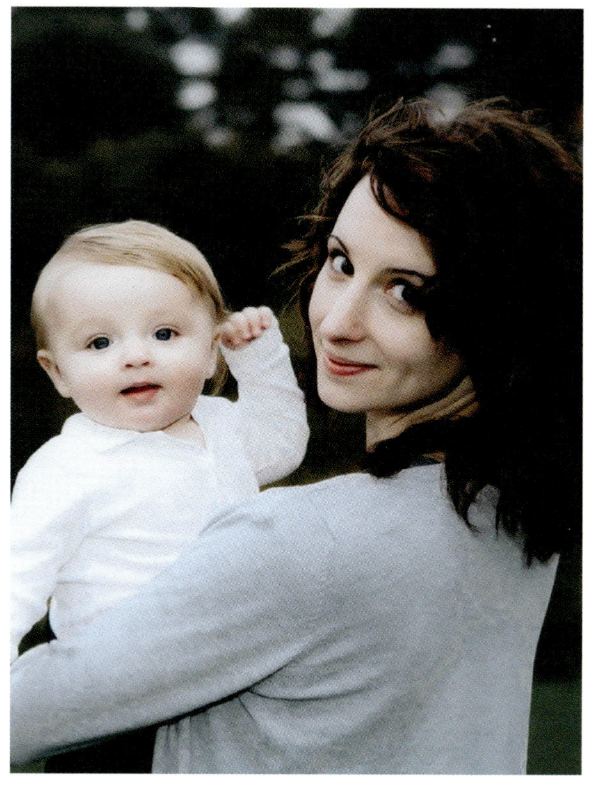

When Charlie was 15 months, we had to fill out a routine questionnaire at the pediatrician's office. The questions asked whether Charlie talked, pointed with one finger, looked in our direction when we called his name, played with us, made eye contact, was interested in other babies, and so on.

Charlie wasn't pointing. He didn't understand little directions I offered. He didn't say "mama" or "dada."

He'd start crying uncontrollably at the sight of another baby or toddler. Looking down at my responses, I started wondering if perhaps something was wrong. But the doctor didn't seem worried and just had us keep an eye on his development. While the idea of it being something more serious briefly crossed my mind, I didn't worry too much about it. After all, I understood a lot of Charlie's behaviors; I, too, liked to be alone, and found eye contact uncomfortable. I figured these behaviors were just part of his personality. Later I learned how important these basic skills are in children's development. I learned that Charlie's behaviors were all early signs of autism.

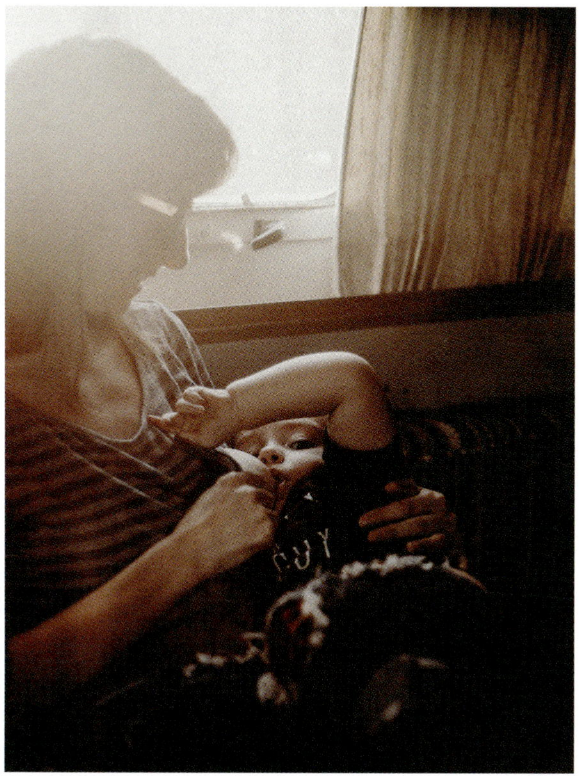

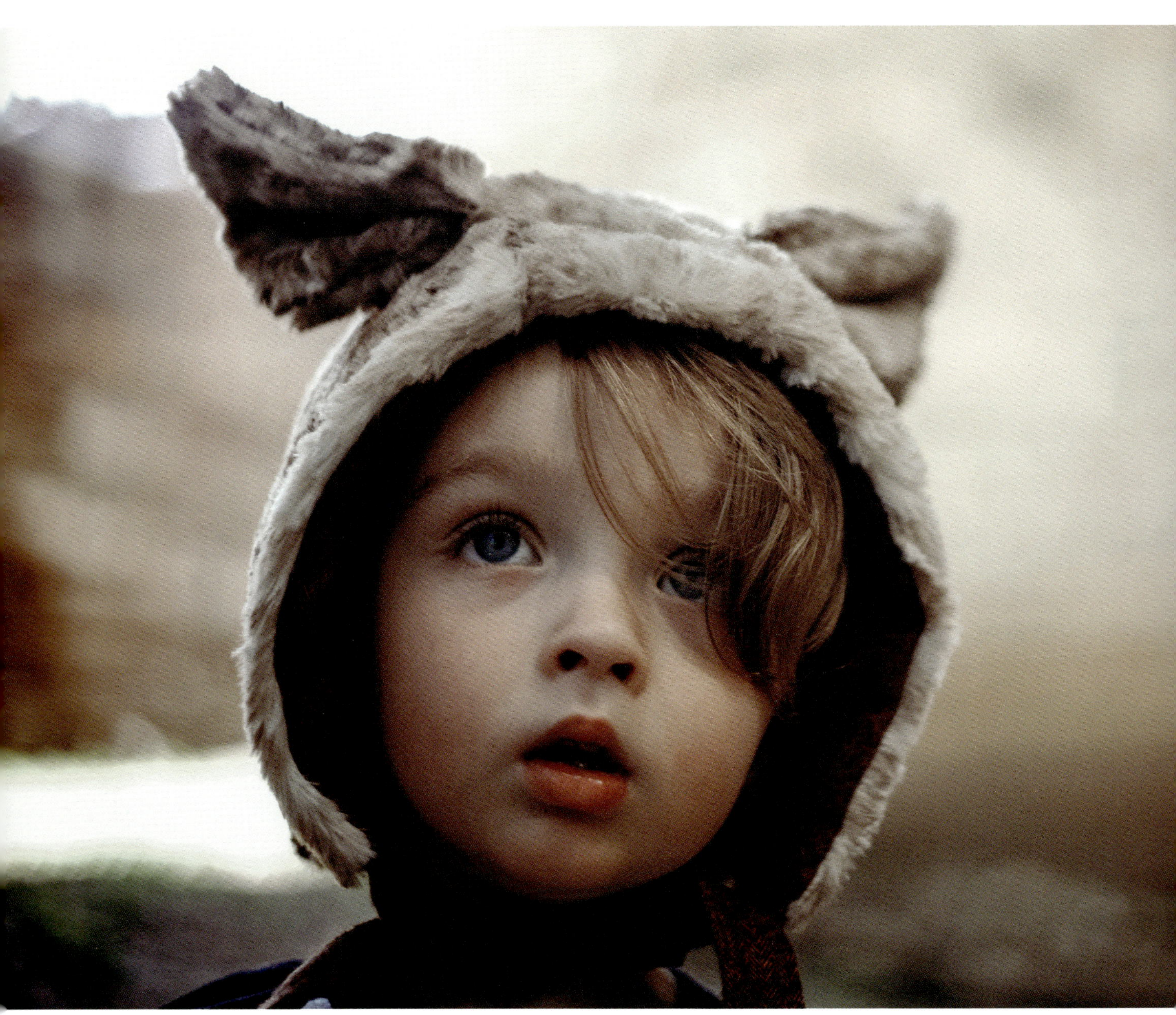

Charlie is obviously not autistic.

At Charlie's 18-month checkup, we filled out the same questionnaire we had at his 15-month appointment. Same old questions, same old answers. Pointing? No. Eye contact? No. Clapping? No. Brings you a rock when he sees one on the ground? No. Points to a plane in the sky? No. Greets you when you come home? Answers to his name? Follows directions? No, no, and hell no. We handed our responses to his pediatrician, but yet again, she told us not to worry because these were routine questions and they were only asking because these behaviors are early signs of autism. And then she said it. She said not to worry because "Charlie is obviously not autistic." She had known Charlie for over a year. She had given him his checkups. She was an expert. So we went home, satisfied.

I wish I had known then what I know now. How could this doctor know so little about autism? After all, 1 in 59 children has autism. You'd think pediatricians would be better trained, particularly because early intervention is key and the earlier the diagnosis, the better chance the child will have to learn key skills and progress. "Obviously not autistic." What did she see in Charlie that made her think he didn't have autism? Or what did she expect to see that she didn't?

After that, things went downhill quickly. I was part of an online mommy group who all had babies born in the spring of 2013, and every week we had a "brag thread." Probably not a great idea in hindsight. I don't know why, but I was there week after week, reading about other moms highlighting their kids' latest achievements. I never felt like I had anything to contribute. Charlie, one of the older kids in the group, wasn't doing any of the things their children were doing.

And then it all happened fast. Over the course
of a few weeks, Charlie started losing the few
words he had until he stopped speaking alto-
gether. I wasn't hearing his sweet little voice
ask me for "de l'eau" or saying "thank you" after
I gave him a cookie. Charlie became completely nonverbal and it seemed as if our connection
was loosening. He didn't like to be touched.

He avoided people, even us, his parents. Something switched and while occasionally, before,
he would sit with us, he now only seemed to
want to be alone. He wouldn't even look at us
anymore, and I was scared. I didn't recognize
my child.

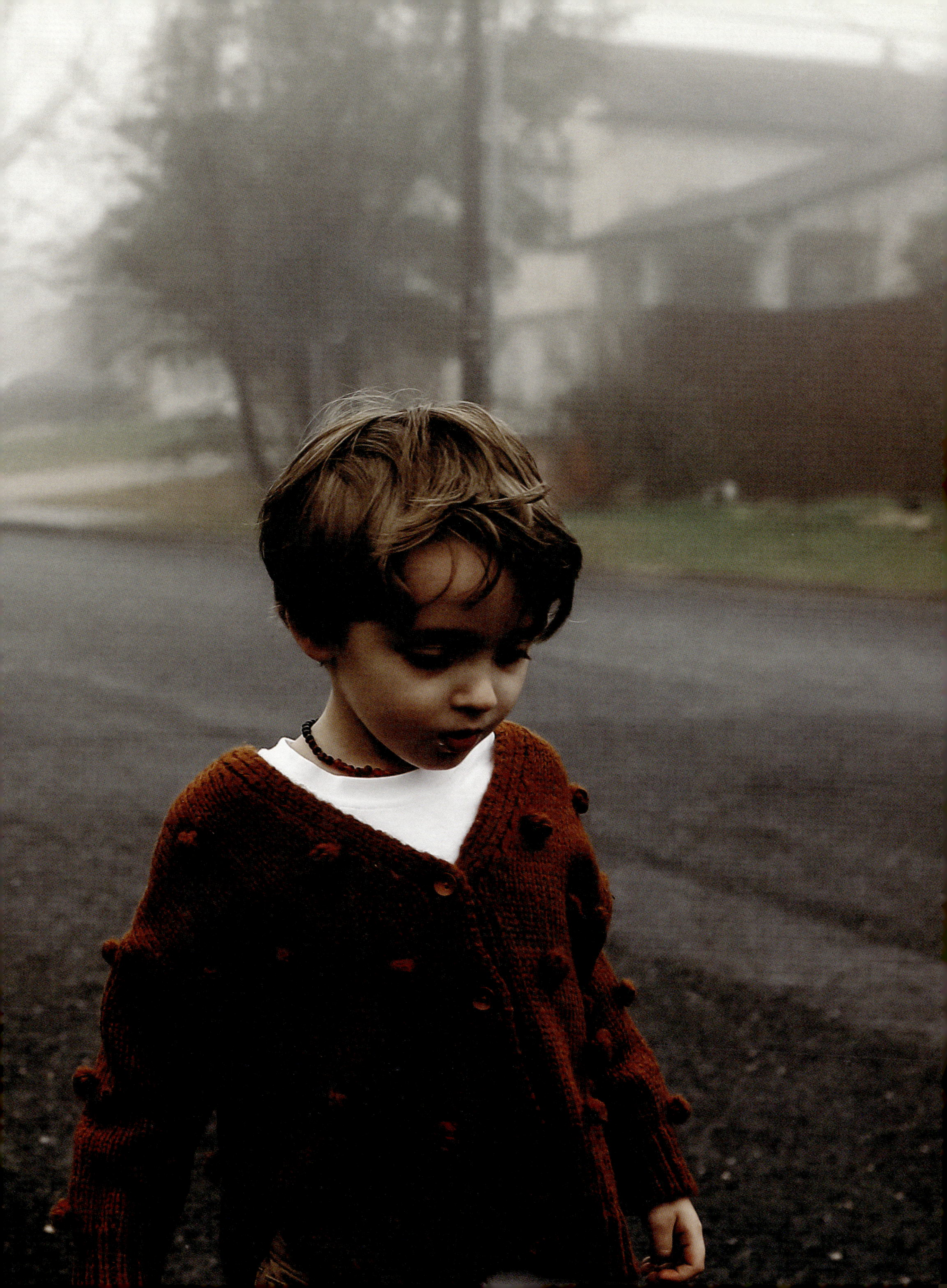

This is when
I started to
understand that
Charlie was really
different; Charlie
needed help.

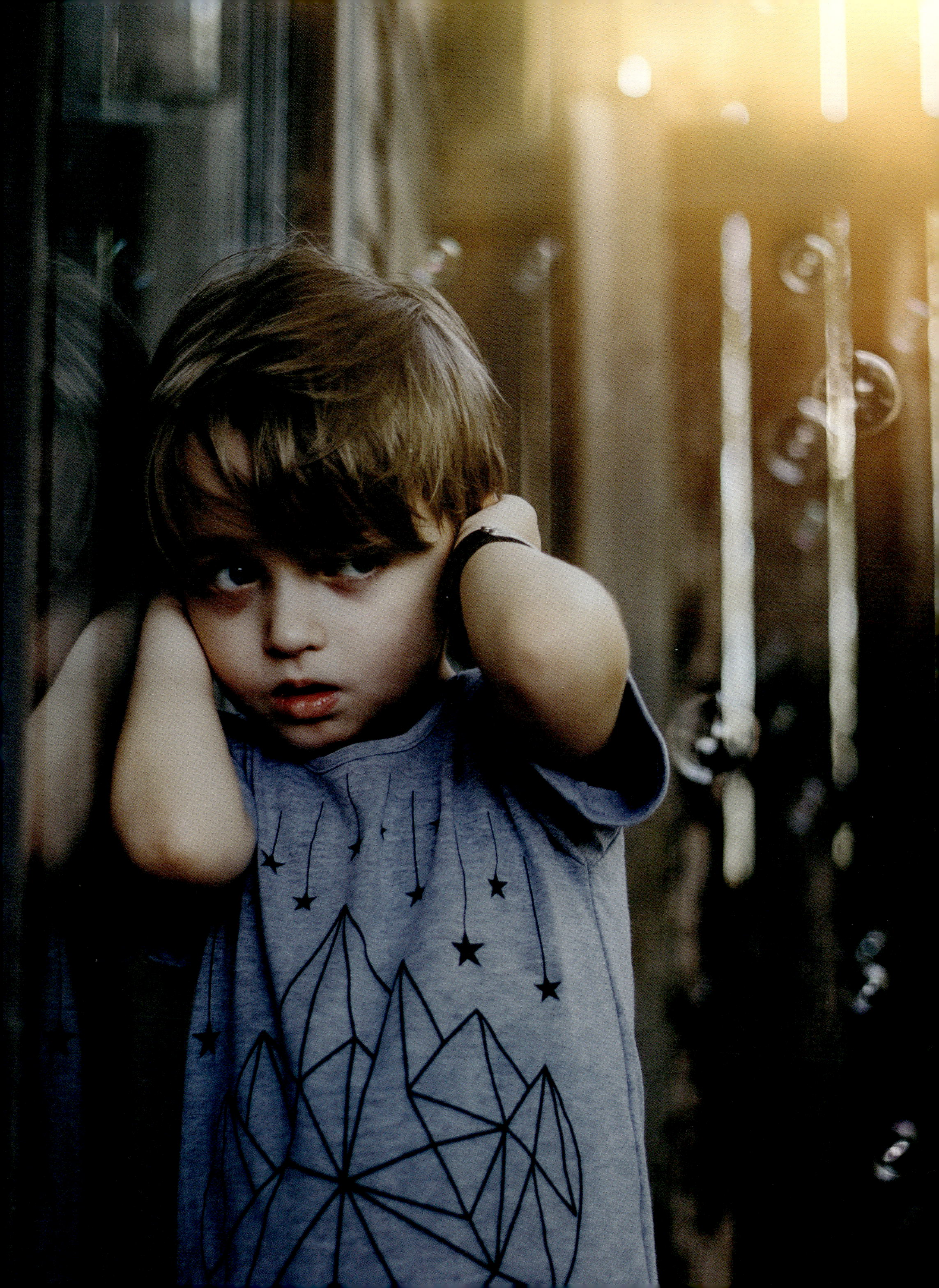

Charlie had changed. I needed to do something. I reached out to a mom I knew from a Facebook group I was a part of whose son is autistic. She recommended that I take the M-CHAT, an online autism screening tool that only takes five minutes to fill out and assesses whether your child is at risk for autism.

The Modified Checklist for Autism in Toddlers (M-CHAT) is available for free on the Internet. It features 20 questions about a child's behaviors, with a range of scores from 0 to 20. A score of 0-2 is considered "low risk," with no follow-up needed. A score of 3-7 out of 20 conveys "moderate risk" and more follow-up questions are asked in the areas where the child showed delays. Charlie scored an 18 out of 20, deep into the "high risk" category where follow-up questions aren't needed and it's recommended you get an immediate referral to a specialist. We didn't know what to do with the information. After all, even though the questions were simple and a doctor administering it would have gotten the same responses, we still believed it couldn't be that serious. The pediatrician had told us a few months ago that she wasn't worried. But my maternal instinct was telling me to do something. So we decided to call Early Childhood Intervention (ECI). ECI is a program available in every state that offers free or affordable therapy for children under three with developmental delays. They came to our home to evaluate Charlie.

This was the first of many encounters with therapists for Charlie. Before they arrived I was nervous, as if this was a job interview. There were three therapists looking back at me when I opened the door: a speech therapist, an occupational therapist, and a supervisor, and they had big bags full of toys. Because we were living in an 850-sq.-ft., two-bedroom apartment, I was self-conscious about how cramped we would be. What did they think about our tiny place? Were they judging us after taking in the ever-present smell of burnt toast that was a mainstay in our apartment? Charlie has always loved toast; I just wasn't very good at making it.

The therapists briefly explained that they were going to ask Charlie to play with their toys and follow simple directions just to evaluate where he was developmentally. Charlie was running around and screaming. I knew right then that he was not going to get high marks. I don't even think he noticed the company in our house. I called him over to see if maybe, for once, he'd come say hi and make a good impression. I wanted Charlie to do well. I wanted the therapists to ask him to build a big tower,

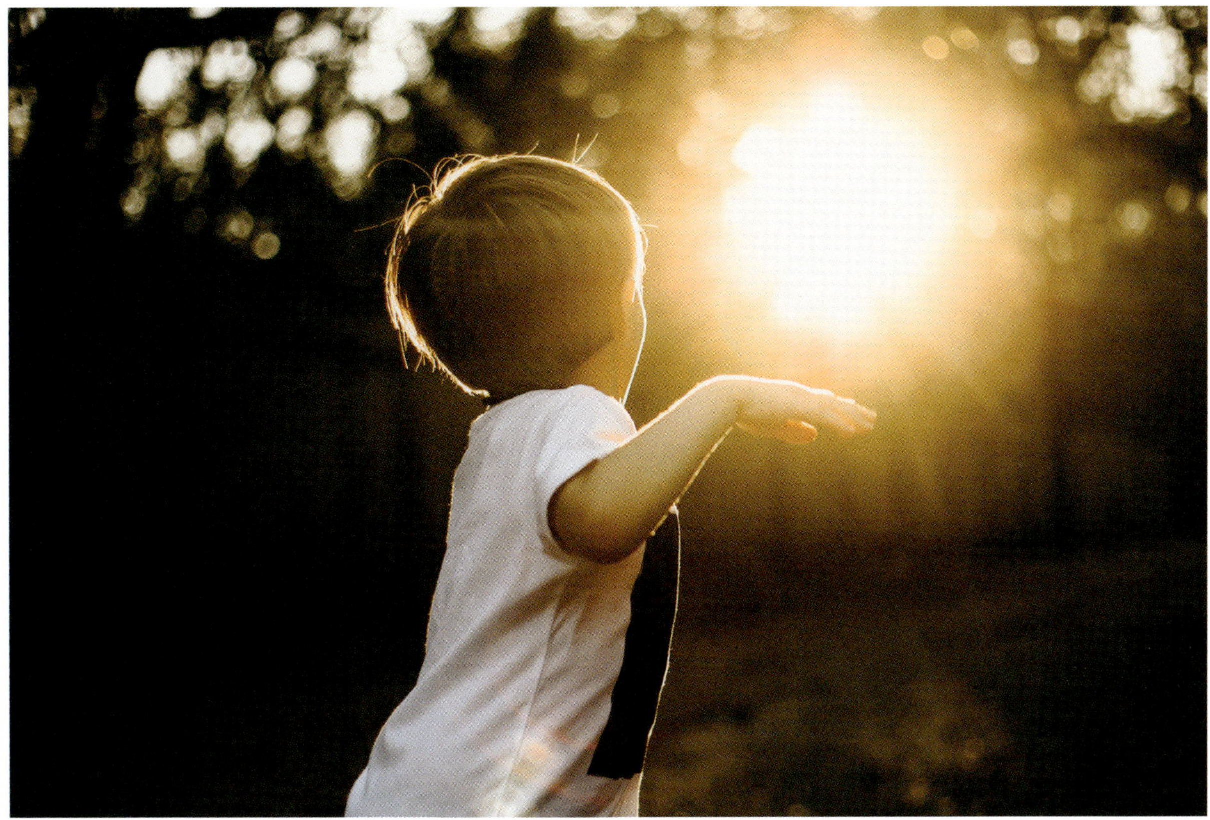

and I wanted them to see how sweet and delicate he was when doing so. I wanted them to love him, but I was missing the point.

The occupational therapist pulled a three-piece chunky puzzle out of her bag and presented it to Charlie. She handed him the triangle puzzle piece, which he threw back at her.

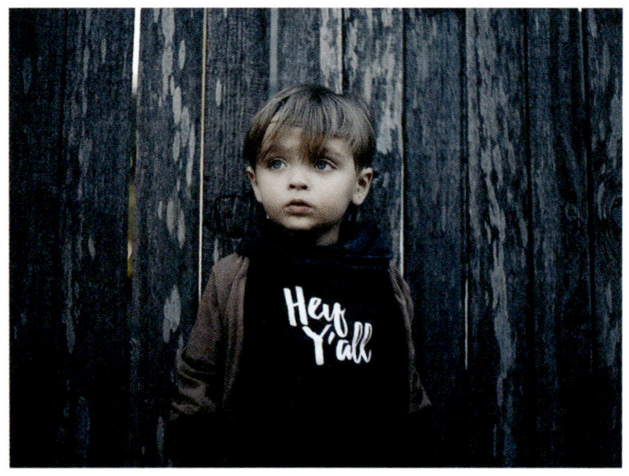

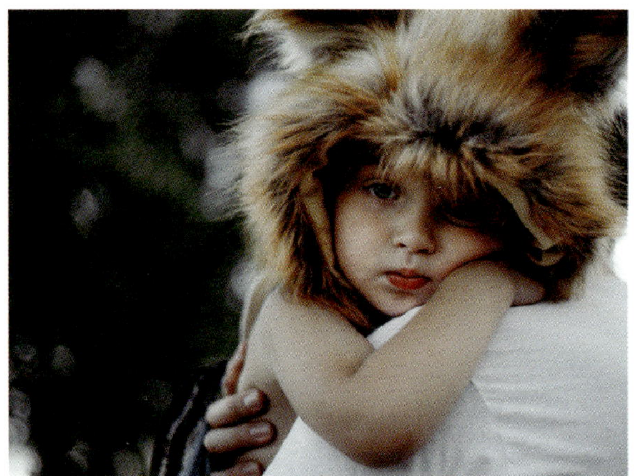

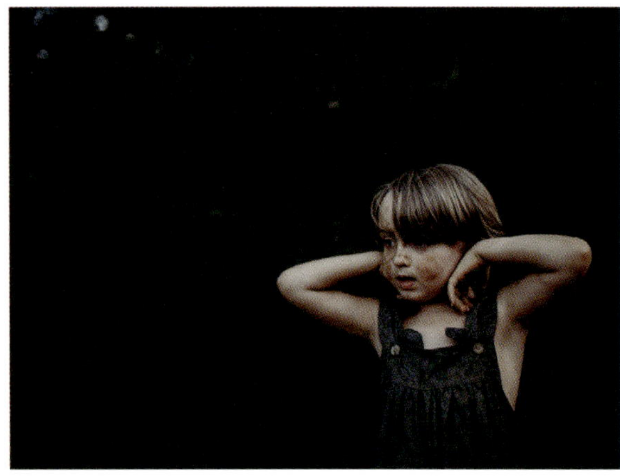

Embarrassed, I apologized while trying to get Charlie to attend to the activity. He enjoyed puzzles and still does, so at the time I thought if there's one test he can pass, this is the one. But Charlie didn't like being told what to do. He didn't understand. He started screaming and crying, and Willy and I exchanged a knowing glance. When Charlie would reach this type of screaming, crying, and kicking, we were usually in for a ride. We kept our calm and offered a bottle to Charlie. No. He threw it back at us.

The therapists decided to skip some of the tests, and with Charlie on the floor between us, they began asking questions. Charlie was so loud that we could barely hear them. I wanted to cover my ears and crawl under a blanket; with each response, the implication of the test became more clear. I'd answered these damn questions a dozen times already, but I gave my responses as calmly as possible, trying not to show anger and to be strong. "No, he isn't pointing." "No, he doesn't answer to his name." "No, he doesn't speak…anymore." "No, he doesn't look at people in the eye." I wondered if I'd ever be able to answer yes to any of these all-important questions.

Charlie was still screaming on the couch next to us, so we turned on Curious George, but cartoons didn't help, either. I started getting lost in my thoughts, suffering in silence and upset that Charlie wouldn't show them the cool things that he could do. The outcome was most certainly going to be, "Your child is indeed severely delayed developmentally." It wouldn't change how I felt for my son, but I started feeling guilty. Did I fail Charlie as a mother? What did I do wrong?! Was it because I ate sushi that one time in my third trimester?

I snapped out of my thoughts as the speech therapist was asking about the temper tantrums, which I thought were a normal occurrence in toddlers. Yes, they happened every day, several times a day, and yes, it was that intense every time. I could see in her eyes that this wasn't normal, and at that moment it sunk in.

Everything would be different. Everything was going to change.

Charlie qualified for every service they could offer him, for Speech Therapy and Occupational Therapy, but they were unable to officially give him an official Autism Spectrum Disorder diagnosis. For that, we would need to see a specialist. ECI provided therapists who came to the house to help Charlie right away. But I came to learn that the amount of time they spent with Charlie, according to experts in the field, wasn't nearly enough. Charlie was to receive two hours of speech therapy, two hours of occupational therapy, and we were offered one hour of parent training per week. This was like throwing a Tic Tac at a starving person. We were reading that the recommendations were anywhere from 15 to 40 hours of early intervention a week. Charlie needed more. Charlie needed someone to advocate for him. He needed someone to get him the help he needed, so I swallowed my pain and started fighting for him.

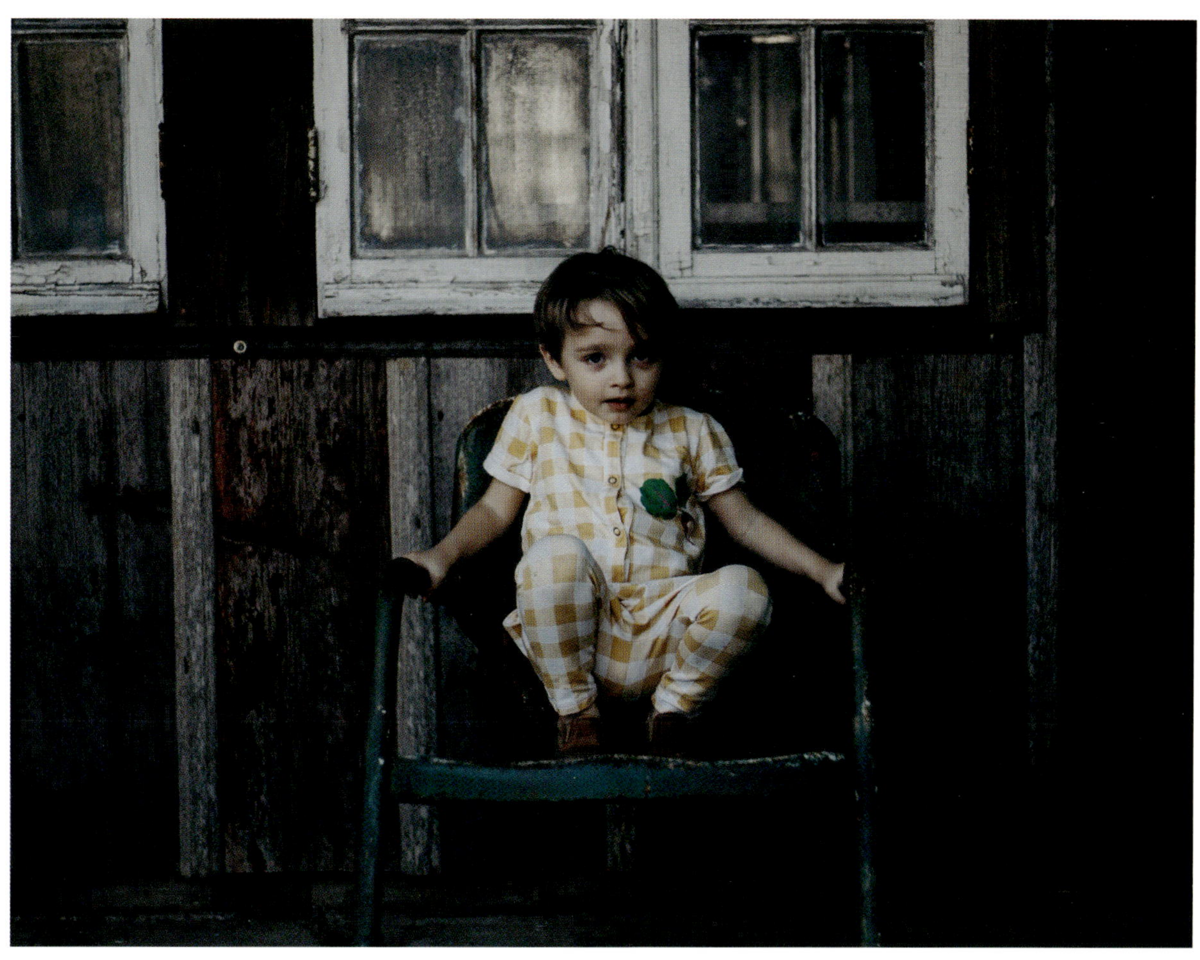

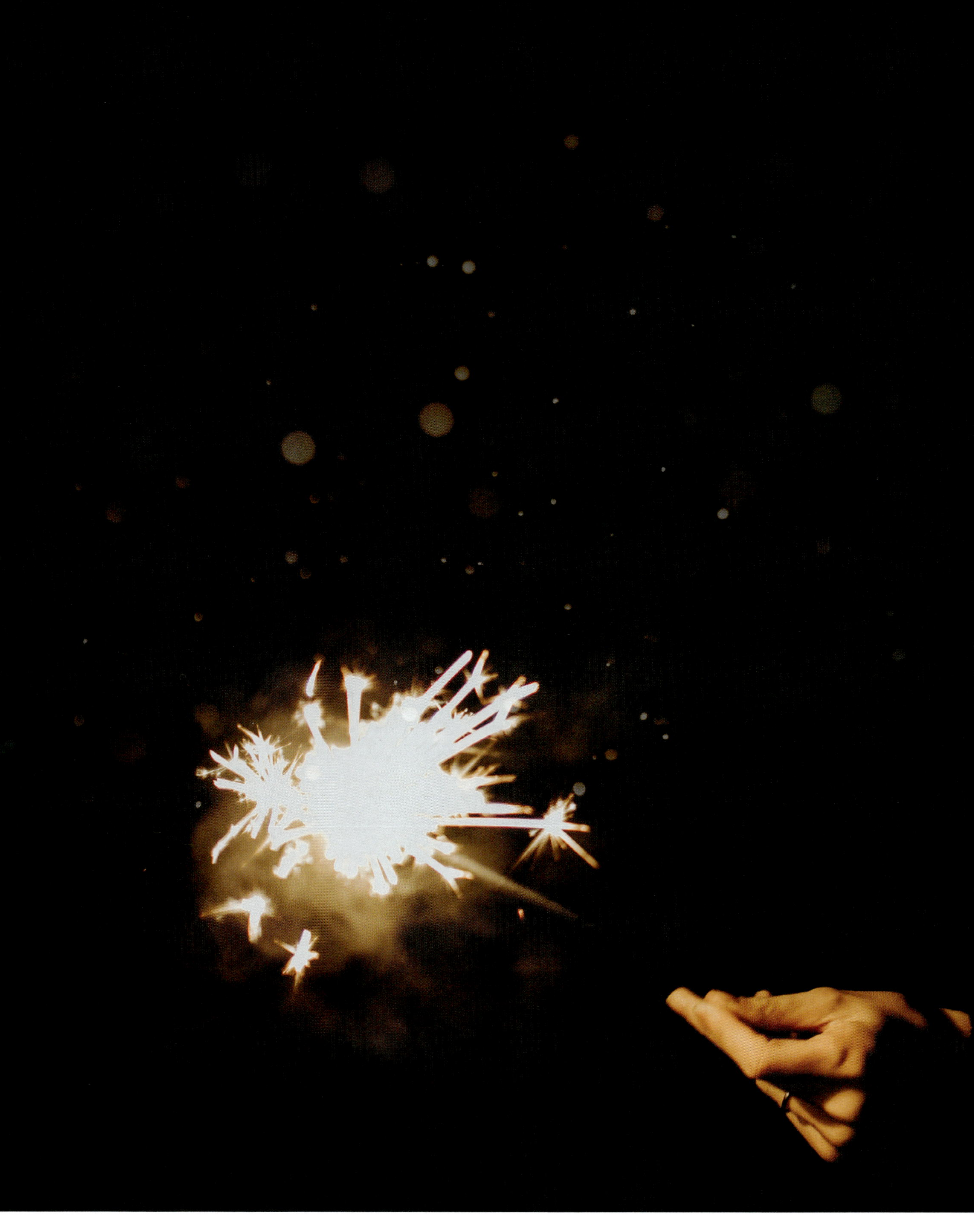

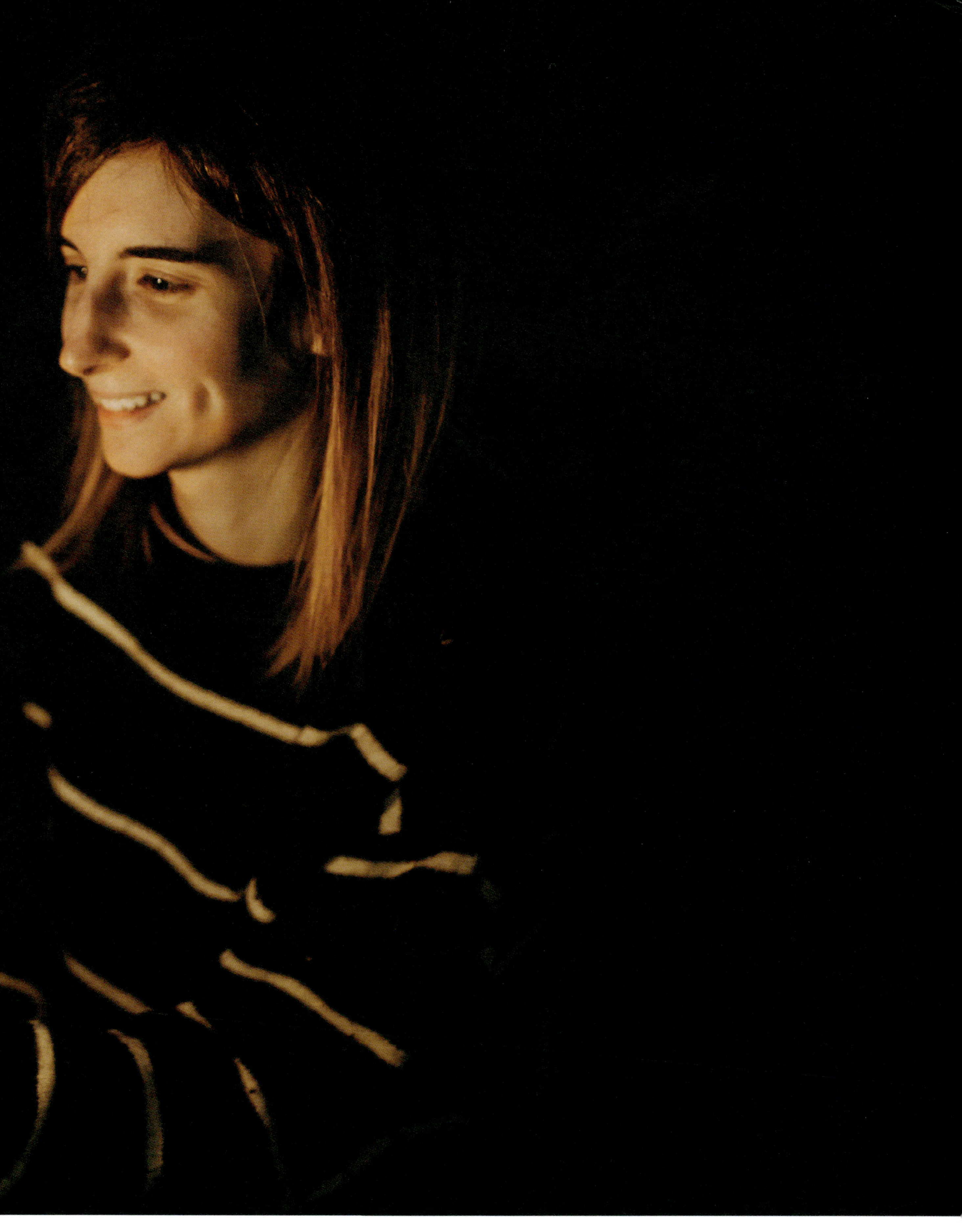

" You walk like a penguin.

"

"Eileen, what did I just say?"

What *did* he just say? I had no idea. I was seven years old, sitting in the back of the class, next to the window, when the teacher interrupted my thoughts. I had been daydreaming about how amazing it would be if one day FIFA allowed women to play on the men's team so I could compete for France in the World Cup. I had also been dreaming about New York City with its yellow cabs and simultaneously thinking about American public schools that I'd seen in movies that looked way cooler than my school in France. There were lockers lining the halls and yellow school buses waiting outside. And I had been thinking about writing a book so that all my ideas and dreams would never be forgotten. Growing up, I had great ideas, many things to say, and big dreams, but no one seemed to understand them. I didn't care if my dreams were unrealistic. They made me

happy. Yet I had a constant, nagging feeling of being misunderstood. Why were kids laughing at me? And why were adults always trying to bring me back down to Earth? Would I one day become a dream-breaker, too?

My *maman* tells me that I've always been different from kids my own age. By the age of three, I had taught myself to read and write. As a toddler, I loved puzzles and memory games which I happily indulged in by myself for hours. But I struggled socially. As I grew up, my mom tried to teach me how to interact with people appropriately by giving me social exercises like going to the bakery to buy a baguette and while there saying "hi," "please," "thank you," and "goodbye." I hated these little exercises. I felt so uncomfortable doing them. It was really hard for me to understand why I was expected to look into people's eyes while saying "hi" to them. I didn't even know them! Strangers would often tell my parents that I was rude. My parents just thought I was shy.

As the years went by, my differences and social struggles became more obvious. It's safe to say that I was picked on a lot. While some are moments I've put behind me, there are a handful of events that truly scarred me. They aren't even the times when I was physically attacked. No, these were the times that I realized what the kids were saying was true.

You walk like a penguin! That phrase still resonates with me, jarring me when I think of it. As I tried to look normal on a basketball court during gym class, a group of kids laughed, calling me "penguin" while awkwardly flapping their hands to mock me. I have to admit that I probably did look like a penguin when I walked. I hated that I was able to see it from their point of view, yet I still questioned it. Penguins' feet face outward, and mine did the opposite. I knew what they meant though: I was awkward-looking.

As I sat on the bleachers looking at my peers having fun together, I wondered if one day I would have that, too. For my entire life, I've felt like I was watching the world through a porthole, disconnected and lonely.

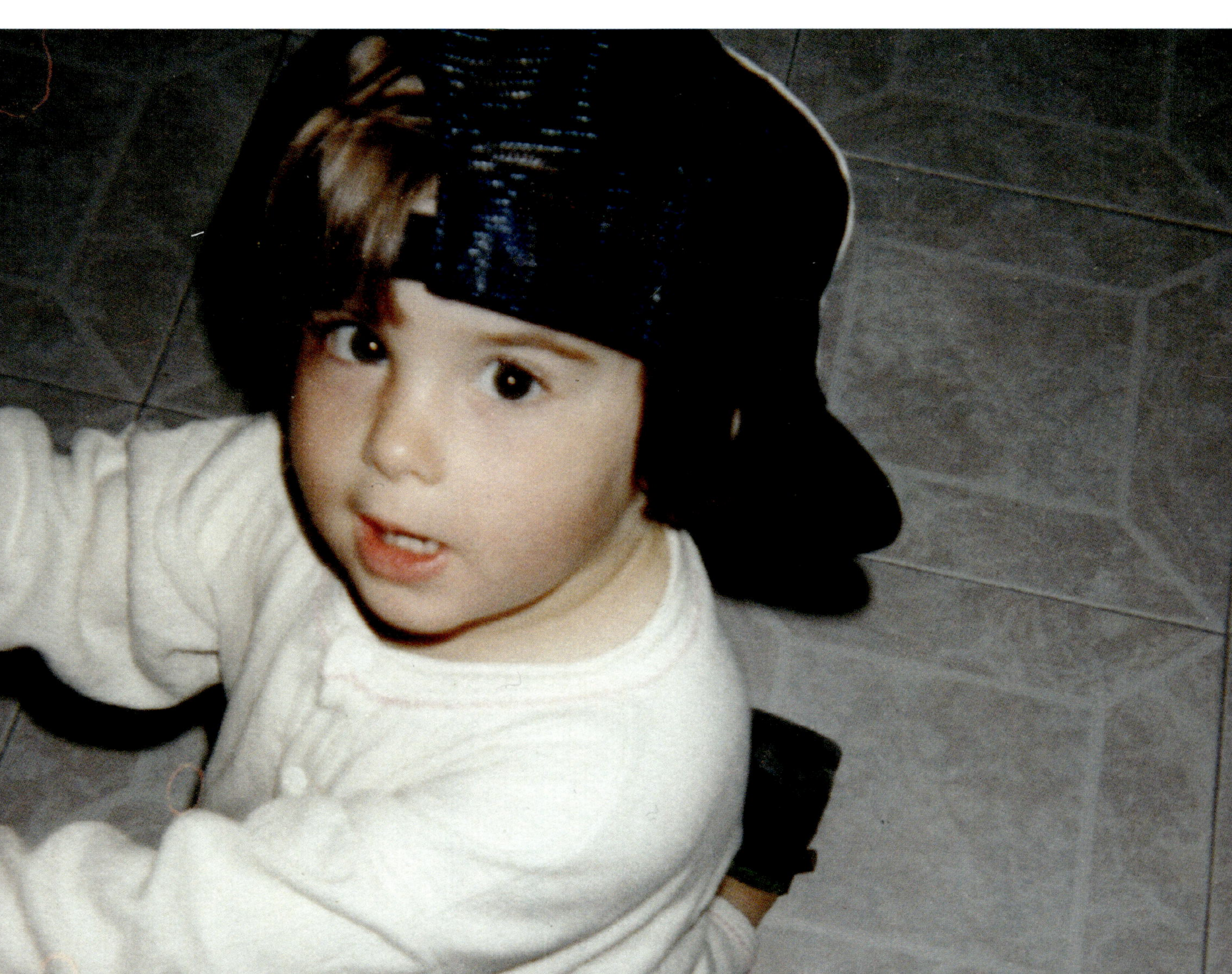

Get Down Now!

In eighth grade, after years of bullying and physical abuse from other children, I found my out—rebellion. I thought that hanging out with the "bad kids" would make me cool, likable. I won't lie: For a short time, it did help a little… belonging to a group was nice. For the first time in my life, I felt accepted. But of course, that could only last for so long.

The "bad kids" were the ones who had more difficulties at school and talked back to teachers. These were the same kids who had mocked me before, so it felt especially good to be accepted by them. I was very gullible and did things that I now regret just to be accepted. Burning a friend's textbook. Tagging walls. Skipping class. Standing up to dance the Macarena in the middle of a lesson to piss off a teacher. Smoking. Talking back to teachers with whom I disagreed. Getting bad grades on purpose to look cool. I knew my actions were wrong, but I longed so much to be part of a group that I did it anyway—to fit in, to belong.

At fifteen I was fully enjoying my new title of rebel. Paying attention in class? Not for me. Getting good grades—who needs 'em? In ninth grade, I had a teacher that would randomly downgrade me because he didn't like my smirk, or *sourire en coin*, which in turn affected my overall score. In France, at the end of the year, each student receives an overall score rather than a set of grades for each class. So these punishments mattered. I don't think it was even legal, but he did it anyway. He wasn't the only teacher to dislike my *sourire en coin* or to punish me for it. There were a few detentions. I was always thought to be sassy when I smiled.

My friends persuaded me to start a "revolution" against my teacher. They told me about that scene in the American movie *Dead Poets Society* where all the students stand on their desk to show their support for their teacher. Loving all things American, it sounded like an amazing idea to me, and being French—well, weren't we the first revolutionaries? So, despite the lack of real purpose, I was sold. We talked about our strategy, set up a time, and my friends assigned me the role of leader. I was thrilled. All I had to do was stand on the table at exactly 10:15 AM, and they would all follow my lead and do the same. At 10:15 AM on the dot, with the teacher right in the middle

PUNITIONS SCOLAIRES - Retenues

PUNITIONS SCOLAIRES - Retenues

I still have my detention slip from this incident…

of a lesson, I took a deep breath and in my Nikes, I climbed up and stood, tall and proud on top of my desk. Except no one followed.

The teacher, baffled, asked me to get down. I didn't. Not right away. Now that I had committed, I was going to do this whether I was alone or not.

It was a mistake. I was humiliated, embarrassed, on display, and completely vulnerable to the swarm of laughter that followed. The ones who weren't laughing just stared at me, wondering what was wrong with the weird girl and why she needed everyone to look at her. The teacher kept asking for my detention book, but I refused to give it to him. I stood there for five long minutes before the teacher called the main office, which swiftly sent the school prefect to escort me to the principal. I got a detention and was also suspended for two days.

Even after all these years, I'd probably do it again, despite knowing now that my "friends" were manipulating me. Because that teacher was unfair. Because there needed to be a revolution. And because it expressed something about me and my life. Me, standing alone, surrounded by my peers making fun of me, and the adults around me either confused or annoyed by my behavior.

Poor thing, you don't have friends?

My love of soccer has always been a big part of my life; maybe to the point of obsession. My hometown, Troyes, has a great professional soccer team. Back when I was in high school and started gaining a bit of independence, I'd go to the stadium after school to watch our players practice every day. Practice was open to the public, and fans liked to attend because the players were approachable and you could ask them for a signature or even take a photo with them. That stadium was a sanctuary for me. I felt safe there.

One day of no particular significance, I was on my way to the stadium to watch practice. I was sitting in the back of the city bus when two tall teenage boys wearing baggy pants and baseball hats got on. I was seated in a section where the two rows of seats faced each other, and the two boys sat in the seats across from me. I didn't look at them, but I could feel them looking at me. I was scared. Something didn't feel right. We were the only people on the bus, except for the driver. I was paralyzed before anything even happened. I kept listening to my mp3 player, The Beatles singing in my ears, trying to look outside to distract myself. Still, I waited for something to happen. And it happened fast. It didn't even immediately register to me what they did. I felt something lightly fall on me, and I looked down to see a bubbly wet spot on my shirt. And as I was looking at it, another one hit. They were spitting on me.

With each spit, they'd loudly clear their throats and essentially do what Americans call "hocking a loogie," but right onto me. I had no idea one could generate so much saliva in a single sitting. I sat there, petrified, unable to move. Where would I go in an enclosed bus? I was afraid they'd hit me if I tried to run away. I just closed my eyes and decided to wait for the next bus stop, an eternity away, so I could run out the door. Meanwhile, the two boys were cracking up and throwing insults like, "Hey bitch, where are your boobs?," and "Poor thing, you don't have friends," or simply "Cunt," while still spitting on me every few seconds.

By the time the bus finally stopped, I was dotted in spit from head to toe. My clothes had changed color from the amount they spit on me. I had never felt so dirty in my life. I was only about a mile away from the stadium, so I just ran straight there. Thankfully, those ass-holes stayed on the bus and didn't follow me.

I was dirty and humiliated, but I had escaped.

As I arrived at the stadium, it started to rain. I was out of breath and still panicked from the situation, so I felt a sigh of relief when I saw someone familiar, the soccer coach of the Troyes team, Jean-Marc Furlan. He was on his way to the field to start practice, but when he saw me running in his direction, he stopped and waited for me. From his perspective, I probably looked like I had been pooped on by a flock of angry birds. He asked me what had happened, and even though I was ashamed, I told him the truth. He was furious and took off his official team practice jacket to give it to me. It was a small sign of compassion, but at the time it meant the world.

I didn't feel this way at the time, but as I've gotten older I can see that in every bad event that happens in life, there's always a lesson to be learned. There's no losing moment; you either win or you learn something. I learned a really simple lesson that day standing there soaking-wet in Jean-Marc Furlan's jacket: Kind-ness does exist.

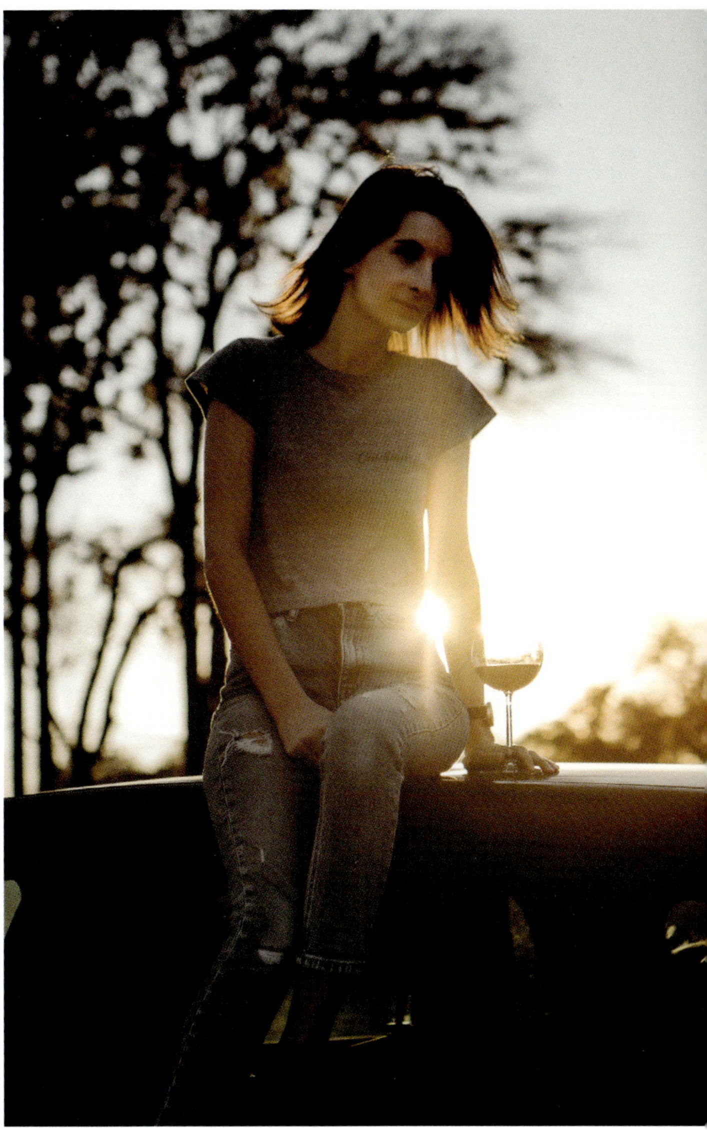

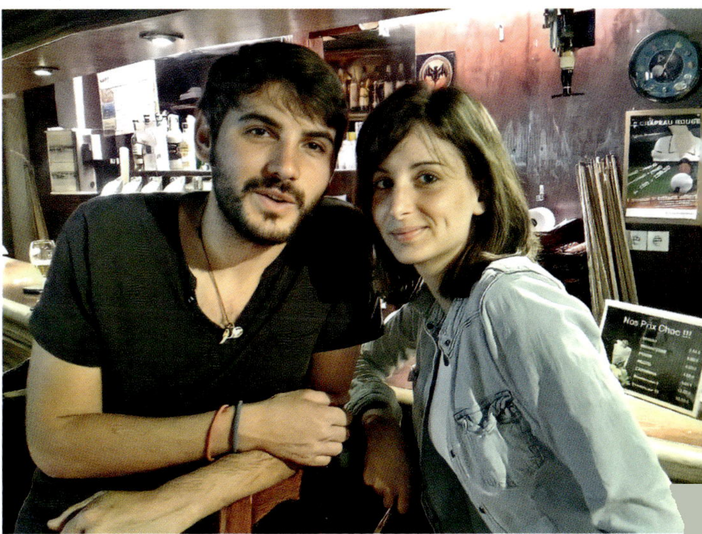

I did have a very good friend, Bastien.

Petition to get Eileen to start wearing a bra.

It's probably not much of a surprise that growing up was hard on me. I had short hair and felt awkward almost always. And then came puberty. Hair in odd places, acne, and uneven boobs, what a trifecta. You'd think that being teased would make me want to dress more like the other girls. I tried not to care about all of that. And even though I made some attempts to fit in with outfit choices, my sense of style wasn't great. I still felt different.

In high school, there were two girls who particularly liked to pick on me. They'd shove me as I walked down the hallway, taking advantage of my generally frail nature and lack of balance. They'd slide out a foot to trip me and even once pushed me down the stairs. I remember them seeming to genuinely enjoy it, which was terrifying.

One day in class, they started passing around a piece of paper from student to student, laughing uncontrollably. "What's so funny?" I wanted to get in on the joke and then it crossed my mind that what was written on the paper might have something to do with me. But I shrugged it off, resisting easy paranoia. It was always hard for me to find the balance between paranoia and naiveté. Finally, the mysterious paper had almost made its way back to me when the teacher noticed it. He grabbed the paper and, unbelievably, read it out loud right then and there. Perhaps he thought he was punishing the author of the note. He read: "Petition to get Eileen to start wearing a bra."

The entire class howled with laughter, just staring at me. The other students had actually signed the so-called petition as it was passed around. The teacher, realizing his mistake, tried in vain to control the chaos. I just sat there, looking down, frozen with embarrassment, and blushing to the tips of my ears. I was furious at everyone, especially the asshole teacher, but also angry at myself for not knowing that I was supposed to wear a bra. I felt betrayed by my mom for not teaching me that wearing a bra would have been a good idea. That day after school, I went to the store and bought my first bra. I'm a quick learner.

I'd love to say this was a one-off torturous moment, but the list goes on and on. And not just in school. Complete strangers felt the urge to insult me simply walking down the street. One time a girl passed by me and just said, "Your hat is ugly." It wasn't even close to being the worst jab I've ever received, but this one stuck with me like a dull physical ache. Teasing had become an actual form of pain. The constant and unexpected nastiness from strangers made me afraid of being myself.

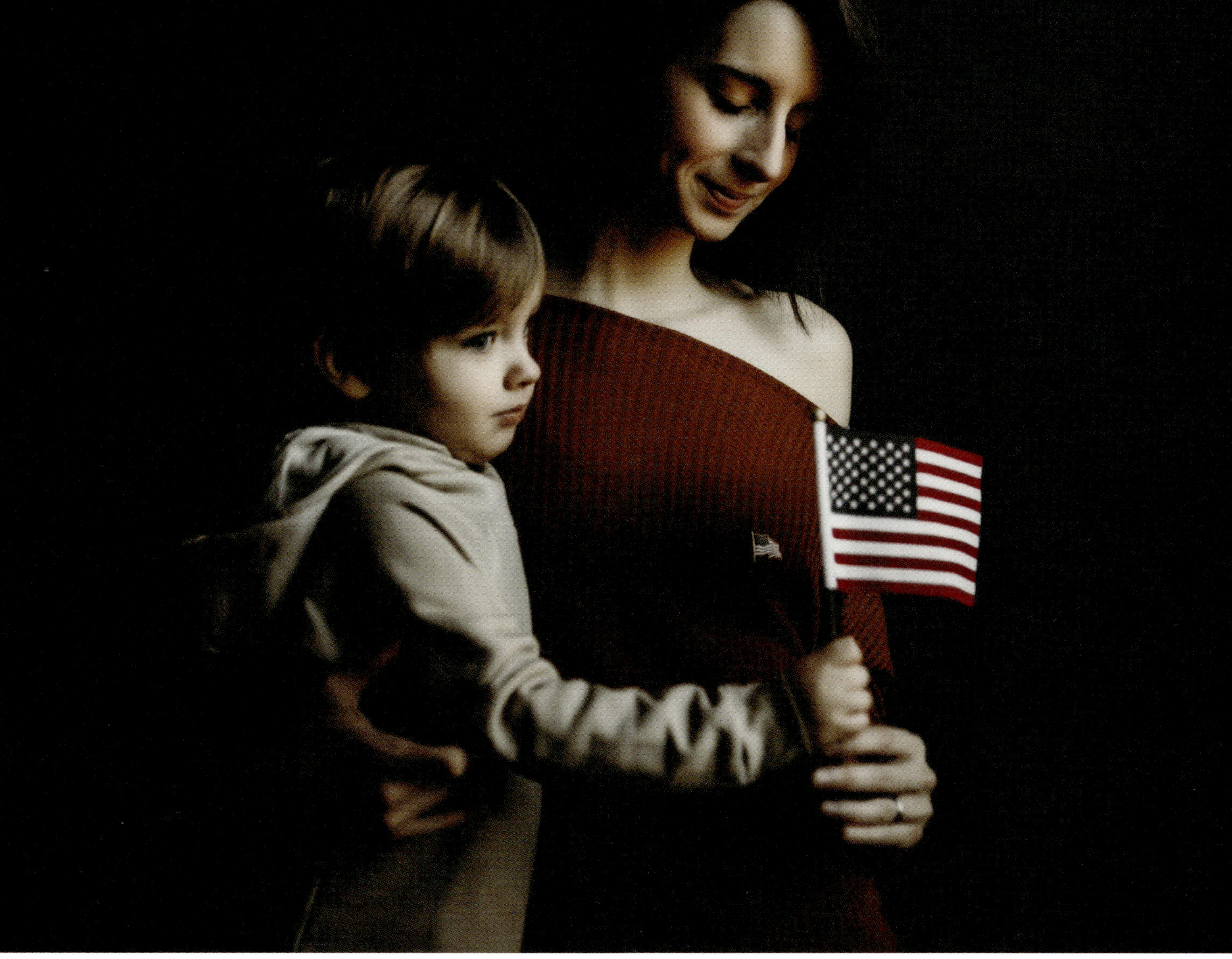

I wanted to get out, to go somewhere far away from France. I craved freedom, a whole new life. I wanted to move to the United States.

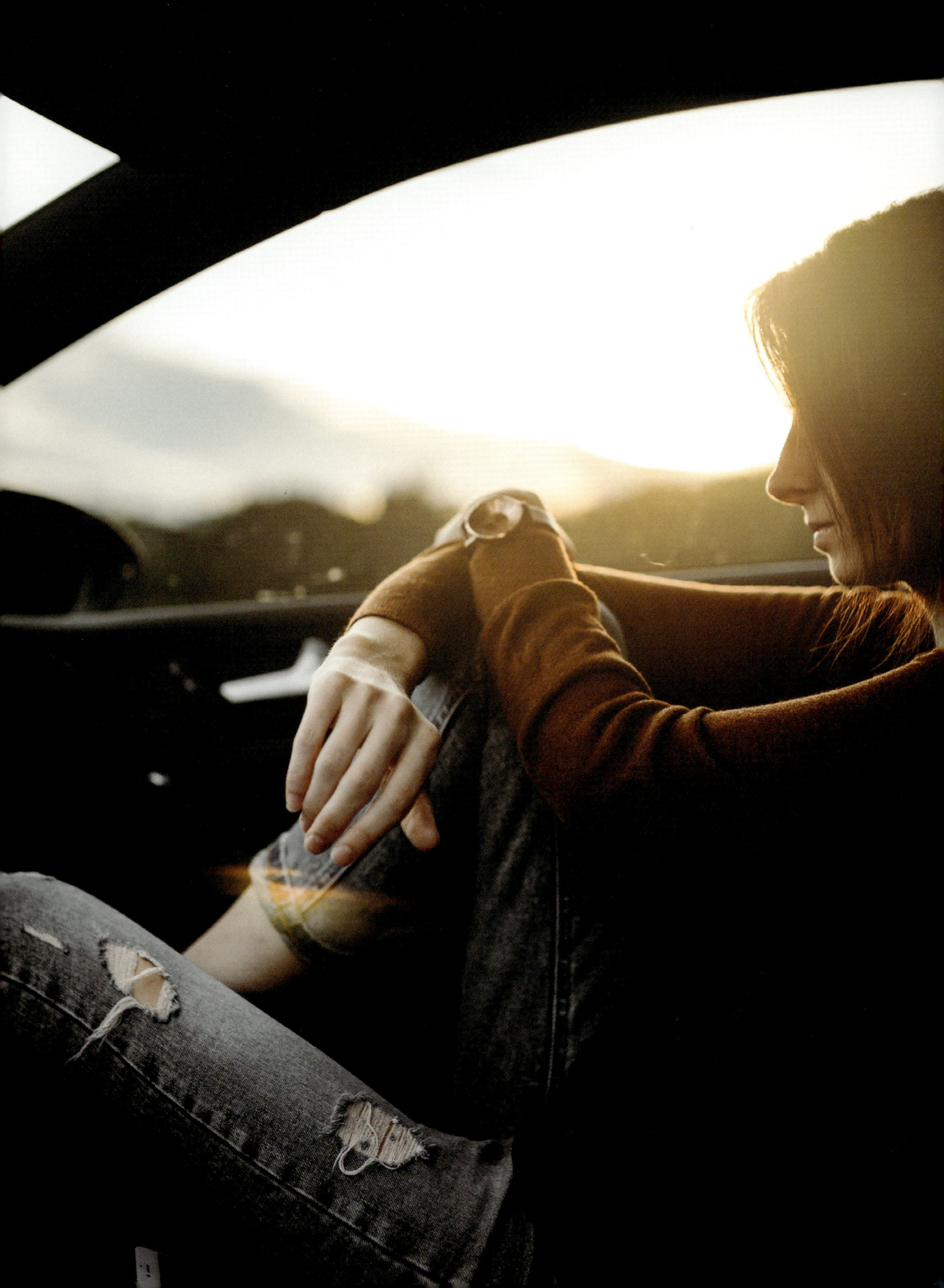

I want to live in the United States.

My mom, who didn't want her only child to leave the country, convinced me to apply to business schools. But I wanted to be an au pair. It seemed like the easiest way to go to the U.S. and learn English. And I liked children. They were easier to be around than adults. School was too overwhelming for me. I tried that already. At 18, I attended the university in Troyes in hopes of getting a B.A. in English. The school was loud and crowded, so as soon as I'd enter the school, I'd get an intense and over-whelming feeling of suffocation. I just couldn't do it. I loved the idea of it, people speaking English in the same kind of auditoriums I had seen in my favorite American TV shows. The reality, though, was quite different.

After two months of torturing myself, I quit. My parents weren't happy with me. I think they missed their gifted child from years ago, the one who was such a natural in school. I don't blame them. By now, they were used to my failures. Year after year, my grades got worse and I wasn't accomplishing anything. I felt like I owed my parents, so to please my mom I decided to apply to both the au pair program and business schools. I always feel a lot of guilt when my actions impact other people, so knowing that going to the USA would break my mom's heart was hard on me. I wanted her to be happy.

I passed the written portion of the tests for a prestigious business school in Bordeaux, the city famous for its great wines. However, the written tests were just the beginning. For official acceptance, you also had to go through an in-person interview. So off to Bordeaux I went. I've always loved traveling by train, looking at the landscapes while listening to my favorite songs. Looking out the window on the train to Bordeaux, leaving Troyes behind, I was happy. Business school started to seem like a good solution after all. I'd still be in France and close to my mom so she wouldn't be too sad, but also far enough away from my hometown that I could start over.

The interview took place at the business school. The place was huge. As big as the large university in Troyes, probably bigger. There were people everywhere, and I began to feel anxious. Once again, I started to feel like maybe this wasn't a great idea. Would I be able to handle the crowd and noise every day?

Upon entering the room I saw that there were three interviewers behind the desk. I wanted to make a good impression, so I put a smile on my face while answering their questions, but they weren't smiling. I couldn't tell what they were thinking, but I instantly got the vibe that they didn't like me very much. They asked me to share one of my dreams with them. I thought that was an awesome question, so I excitedly told them: "I want to live in the United States." They laughed. Why did they think that was funny? Did they want me to answer "world peace"? I left knowing I wouldn't score high enough to be accepted. Still, I waited patiently for the results, holding onto the hope that I would somehow obtain a passable score and get in. Two weeks later, a letter arrived with my interview score of 4/20 (a four out of twenty!) and a rejection from the school. They really didn't like me.

To top it off, I wasn't matching with any families on the au pair website. I had posted a video of myself speaking in English with my strong French accent, telling host families a little bit about myself. I emphasized my love for soccer and good cuisine. Over the course of the summer, only one family in Los Angeles showed any interest, but after we chatted on the phone, that was the end of that. A little stung and with no plan in place for the fall, I was feeling even more anxious about my future.

A few weeks before the first day of school, my mom pushed me to attend the in-person interview at another business school in my hometown. Of course, I didn't want to go, but I went for my mom. That, and I had no other options. This time surprisingly, I did pass. But not a single morsel in my body was excited about it. I would drown in a business school, I would fail. I knew I needed to find the courage to walk away.

The constant, nagging need to move to the United States kept me moving forward.

I would find a way to make it happen.

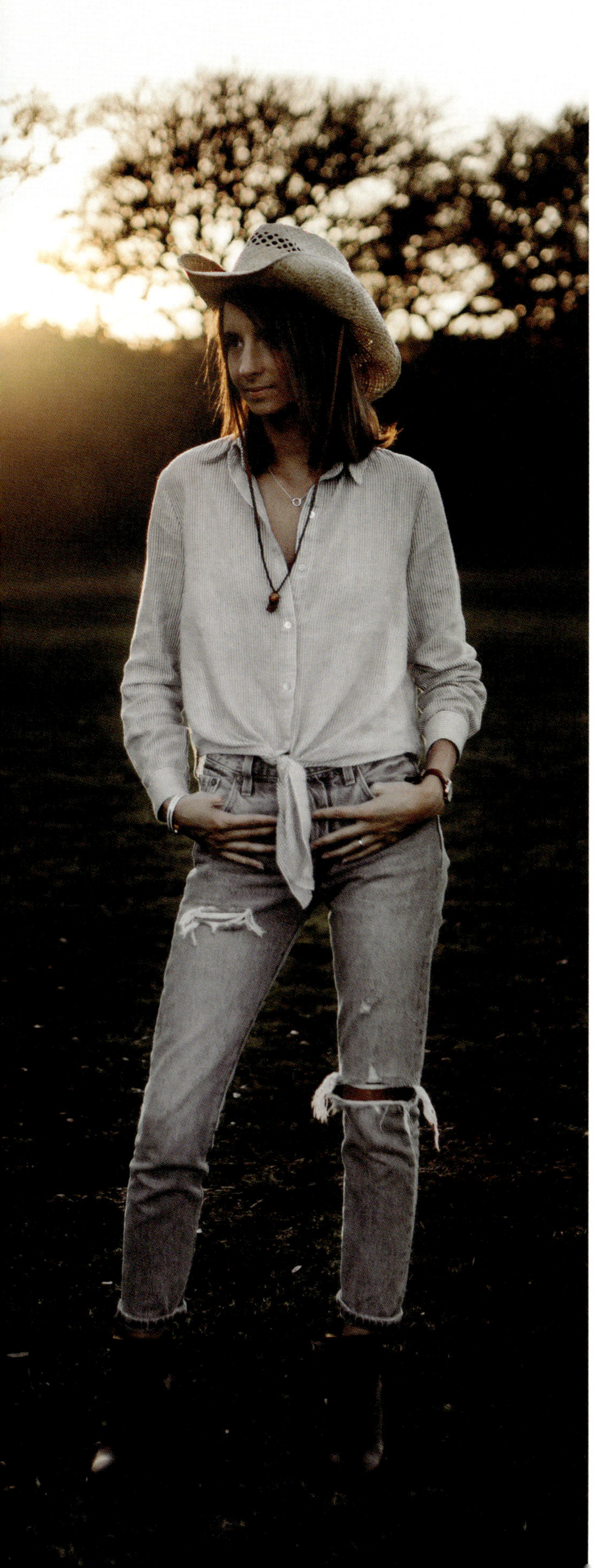

Howdy, Cowboy!

Maybe when you wish for something hard enough, it comes to life. I don't know. Maybe it's the universe steering you in the right direction for your journey. But the day after I received acceptance into that business school, I received an email that changed my life. I had an au pair match with a family in Austin, Texas, and they wanted to chat with me on the phone. I was ecstatic. Texas! From my French girl point of view, Texas was exotic and super cool. I was under the impression that almost everyone there wore cowboy boots and Stetson hats and rode their horses to the store while greeting others with a "Howdy, Cowboy!" Super accurate stereotype, obviously.

My video interview with the family actually went well. We talked about music, cuisine, and sports. To my huge surprise, they weren't wearing cowboy hats or boots. I was able to understand their English, and that made me feel proud. I had a great feeling about them as soon as we met on Skype. They told me that Austin was the "live music capital of the world," and as a music lover, I was very excited about that!

They had a little boy who loved soccer, and that's why my video had caught their attention.

This sweet family seemed like the perfect match for me. But I couldn't tell them yes right away as much as I wanted to. Because there was still my mom to think about. She was heartbroken at the thought of me leaving for a year to live across the world. "What am I going to do without you?" she kept repeating. The guilt was overwhelming, and I felt a responsibility to stay.

That Sunday night, before the first day of school, I kept tossing and turning in my bed, unable to sleep for long hours. I got up at 6:00 AM, in a fog from the lack of sleep, and found my mom drinking her coffee in the living room. She was smiling, and I knew what I was about to say would break her heart. I told her, "I'm sorry, but I can't. I'm not going to school today. I'm not happy here. I'm going to Texas for a year. I'm sorry."

She cried and I kept apologizing because I was sorry to be hurting her. But I wasn't sorry for wanting to leave. I wanted to see more of the world, I wanted to be excited about life. The kind of life that makes you want to get up in the morning with a smile. In my mind, I had already left. I would take my life into my own hands. "It's just for a year" I kept repeating. "And there's Skype, and email, and WhatsApp." More tears.

The weekend before I left, I had a going-away party at the bar with the few friends I had left. We all wore cowboy hats, plaid shirts, and fake guns on our belt—very American. It felt like a real turning point like I couldn't see what lay ahead, but I knew this life was already in the past. People were joking that I'd find an American boy and never come back. They didn't know how true that would turn out to be.

People often ask me why I left France, and I don't really know what to say. I'm almost afraid to ruin their fantasy, that romantic image of a country idolized by so many. To sum it up, France and I just weren't meant for each other. To this day, we remain friends, but from afar. I love France, as long as I don't have to be with her every day. The constant judgment from strangers and the stigma around mental health and disability were just too much for me. Even as I write this, I can't help but feel that France failed me. It took my mom saying these words for things to click into place: "Charlie can't be autistic. You were the exact same way as a child." What if I've always felt different because I actually was? What if there was no place for me in France because of the French attitude about difference, about disability, about autism? One year after my mother spoke those words, I sought a full therapeutic assessment to try to get some answers.

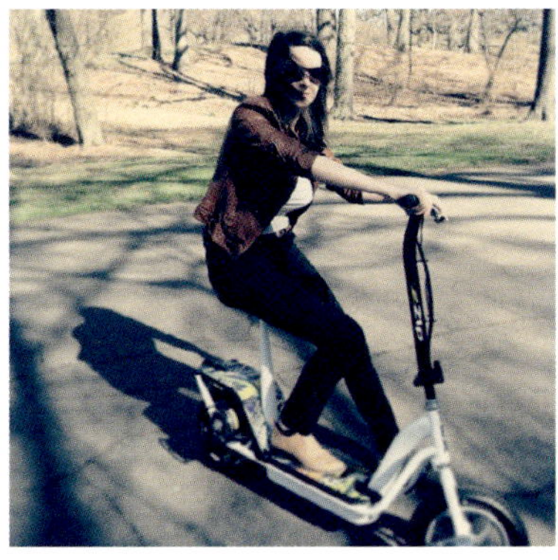

In Austin, there was a coffee-house near my host family's house that had a big outdoor patio and a stage where local musicians came to play music weekly. It felt like a place where I could just be myself. The people were friendly and always smiling. It reminded me of the community I had in France at the bar. I felt in my element and like I could be myself without fear of being judged.

I'd find myself walking a mile or so to the coffeehouse most days after work just to have something to do. It wasn't that I didn't know how to drive; I had an international license. My host family just wouldn't allow me to drive before I'd passed my American driving test. When I took my driver's test in Texas, my rusty parallel parking skills earned me a big fat F, not once but two times in a row. To this day, I still have no effective method for parallel parking. I remember once in France "borrowing" my mom's car to go to the bar. After a long minute of maneuvering, I finally managed to park in a relatively tight spot at the bar, and people proceeded to clap and cheer as I got out of the car. I was mortified on the inside. But being the good French girl that

I was, I hid my embarrassment and took a bow, thanking the strangers for their ovation.

Living in Austin and being without a car isn't the most practical way to get around. I couldn't very well walk everywhere I needed to go. After seeing a child ride an electric scooter through my neighborhood, I immediately decided that it was an amazing idea and that I needed one. I searched Craigslist for a used scooter and found one. No, it wasn't a Vespa or something cool or sleek-looking. It was an electric scooter for children and had a maximum speed of 12 miles per hour with a tailwind. Tex, as I had lovingly named my scooter, was loud and would break down every other week, but I'd fix it every time. Man, I loved that thing. It became part of my identity in Austin. Eileen and Tex. I would ride around on my child's scooter with my helmet on and it must have been a pretty funny sight to see because people always smiled at me when I drove past them. It's one of the things that made me fall in love with America: People will smile at you on the street and then continue on with their day. Just a small gesture that says "I see you."

One day after work, I pulled into that coffeehouse I loved so much when a good-looking guy said something to me as I was taking off my helmet. "You must pick up a lot of chicks with that scooter." Was he talking to me? I looked up and saw that he was, but I couldn't have been more confused. "What? I'm French," was the only thing I could think to answer. Why would this guy want to talk to me about his chickens? He smiled and repeated some nonsense French phrase about an umbrella and a pencil sharpener constructed from words he'd

remembered from a high-school French class, and we started talking more from there.

Willy. Handsome guy, I thought. He looked like a young Justin Timberlake and was carrying a guitar around his neck.

We sat talking about nonsensical things and bonded over our love of music. I liked him because he struck me as different and funny, and I felt like he wasn't bothered by my quirks. I was actually at the coffeehouse to meet my then-boyfriend for a chess game. So I let Willy know I had a friend arriving soon, and he left. I was so bummed when I realized that I might never see him again. A little while later, while I was in the middle of my chess game, Willy came back into the coffeehouse and pretended to be waiting for a friend at the bar. I tried not to look up too often and meet his eye, but I couldn't help from smiling inside wondering if he was looking at me. I guess he got antsy and obviously didn't think much of my boyfriend, because finally he just came over and sat down right at the table with us. This guy's got some balls, I thought! We're now married with two kids, Charlie and Jude.

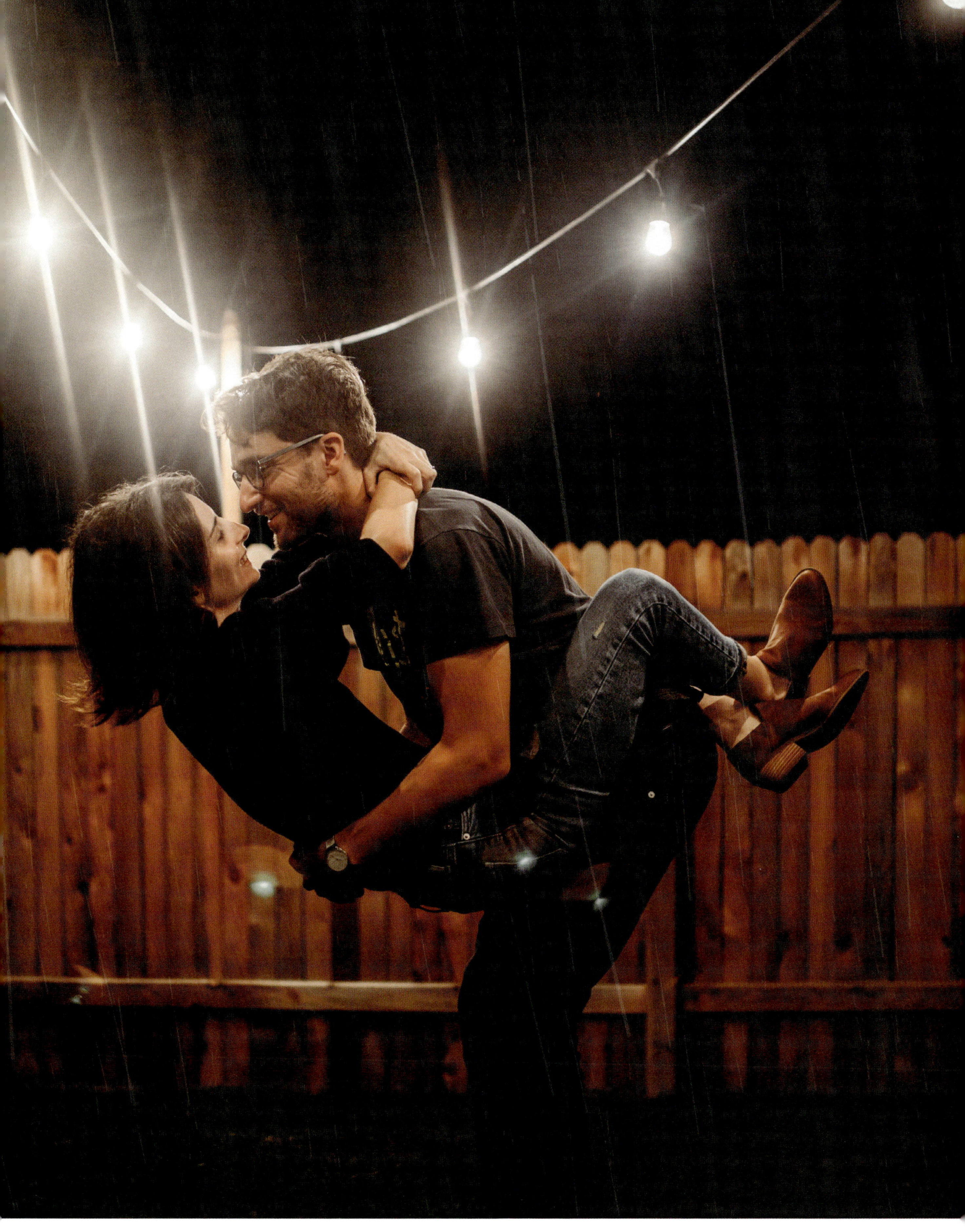

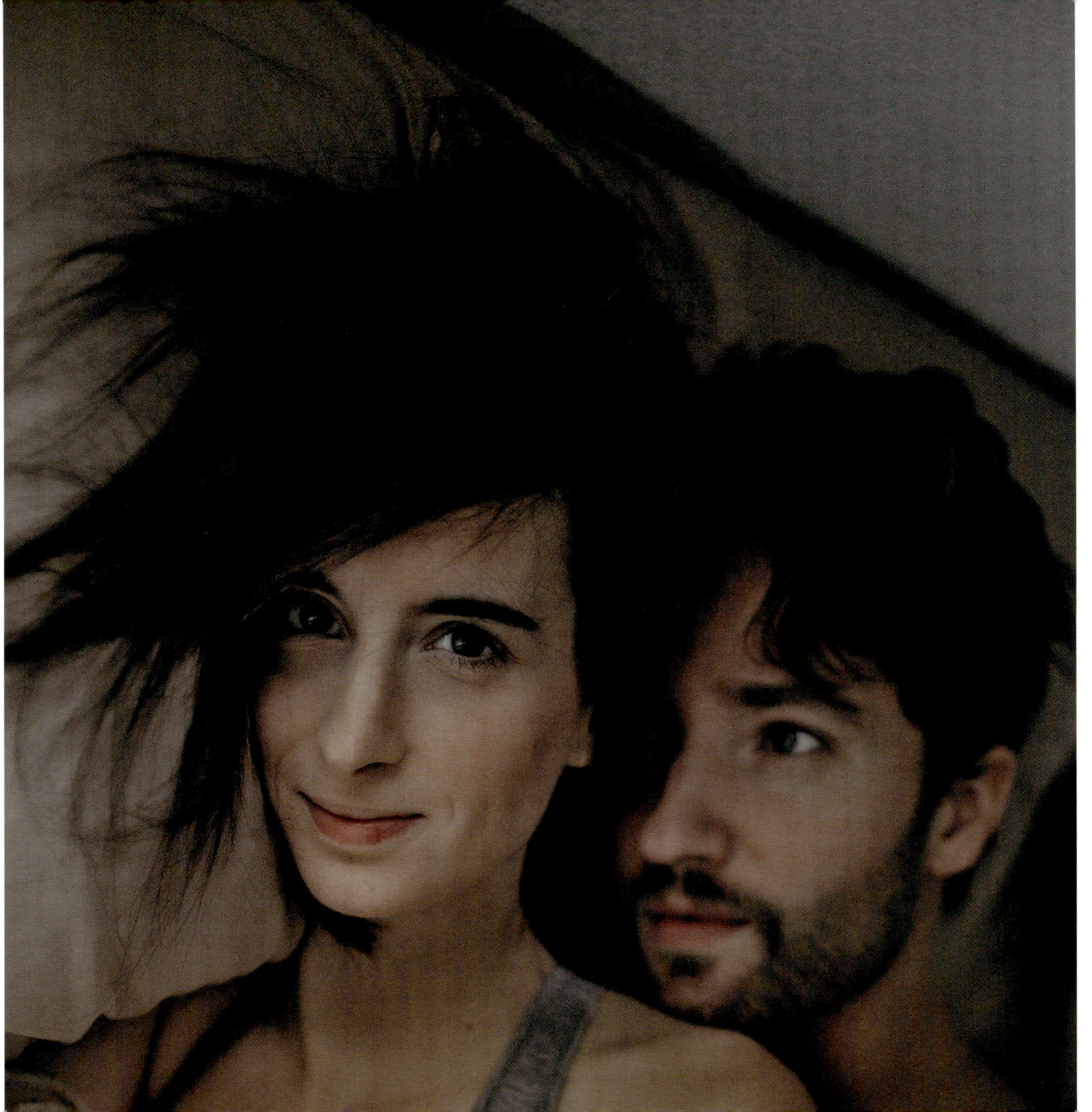

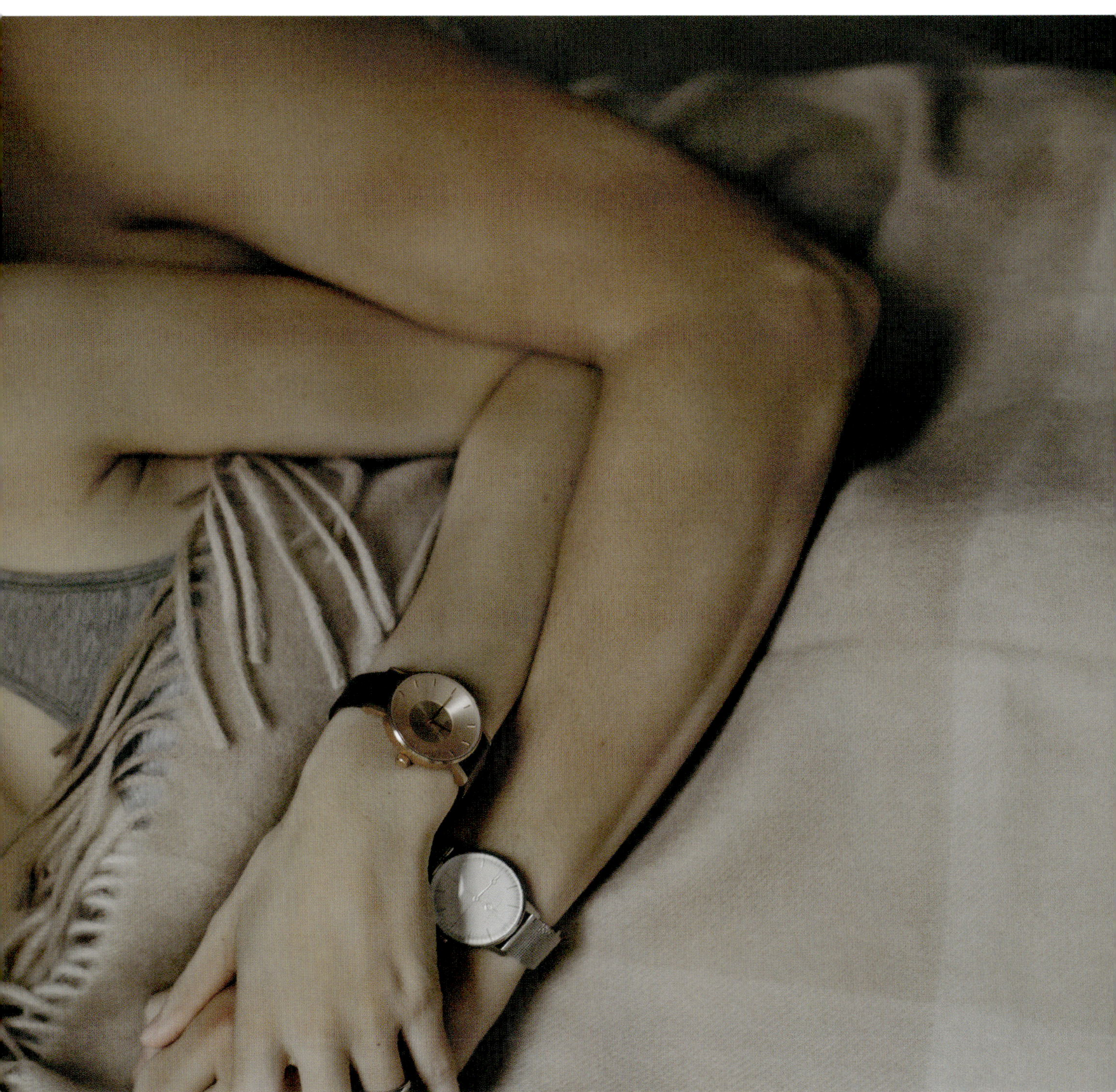

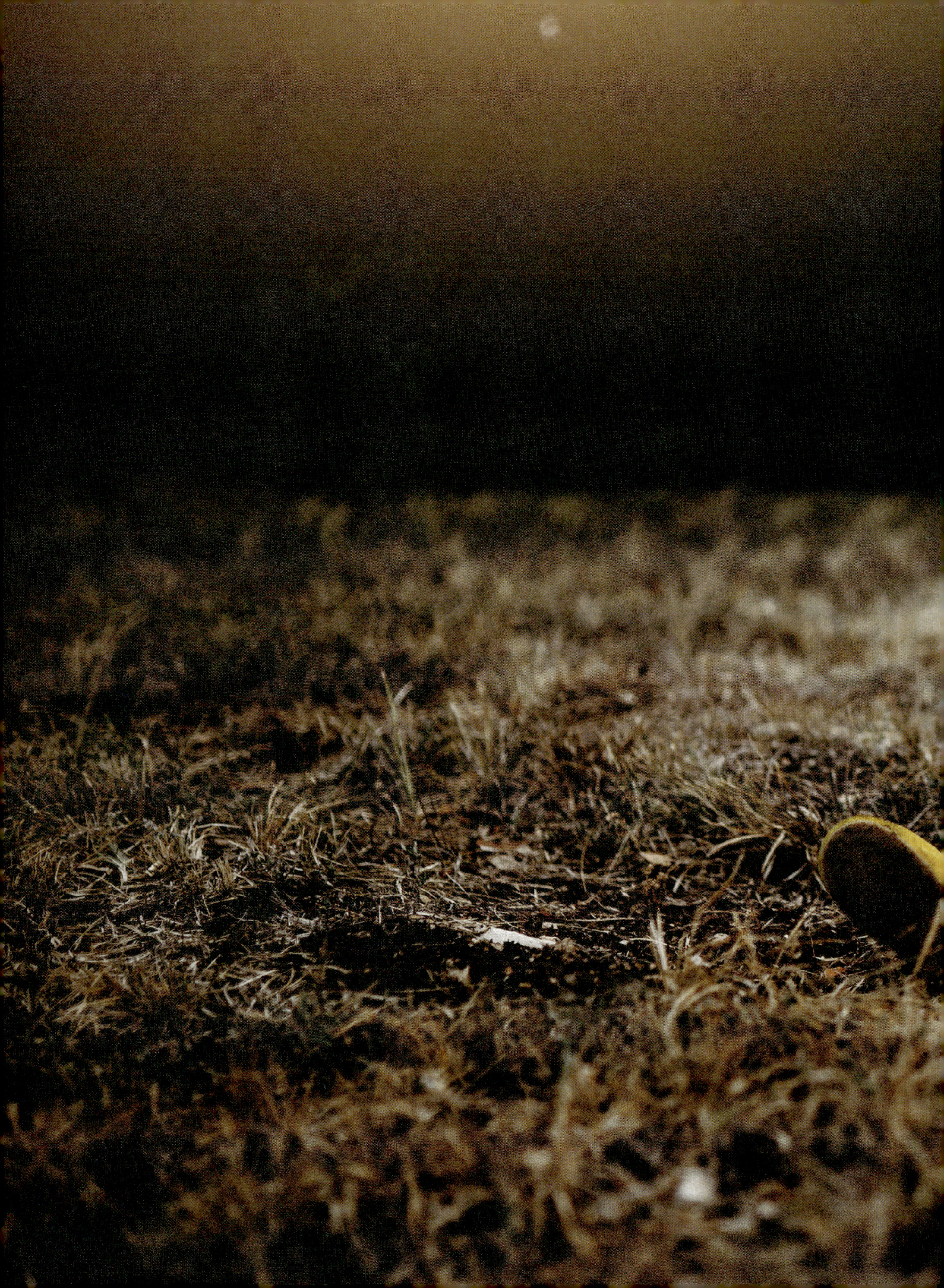

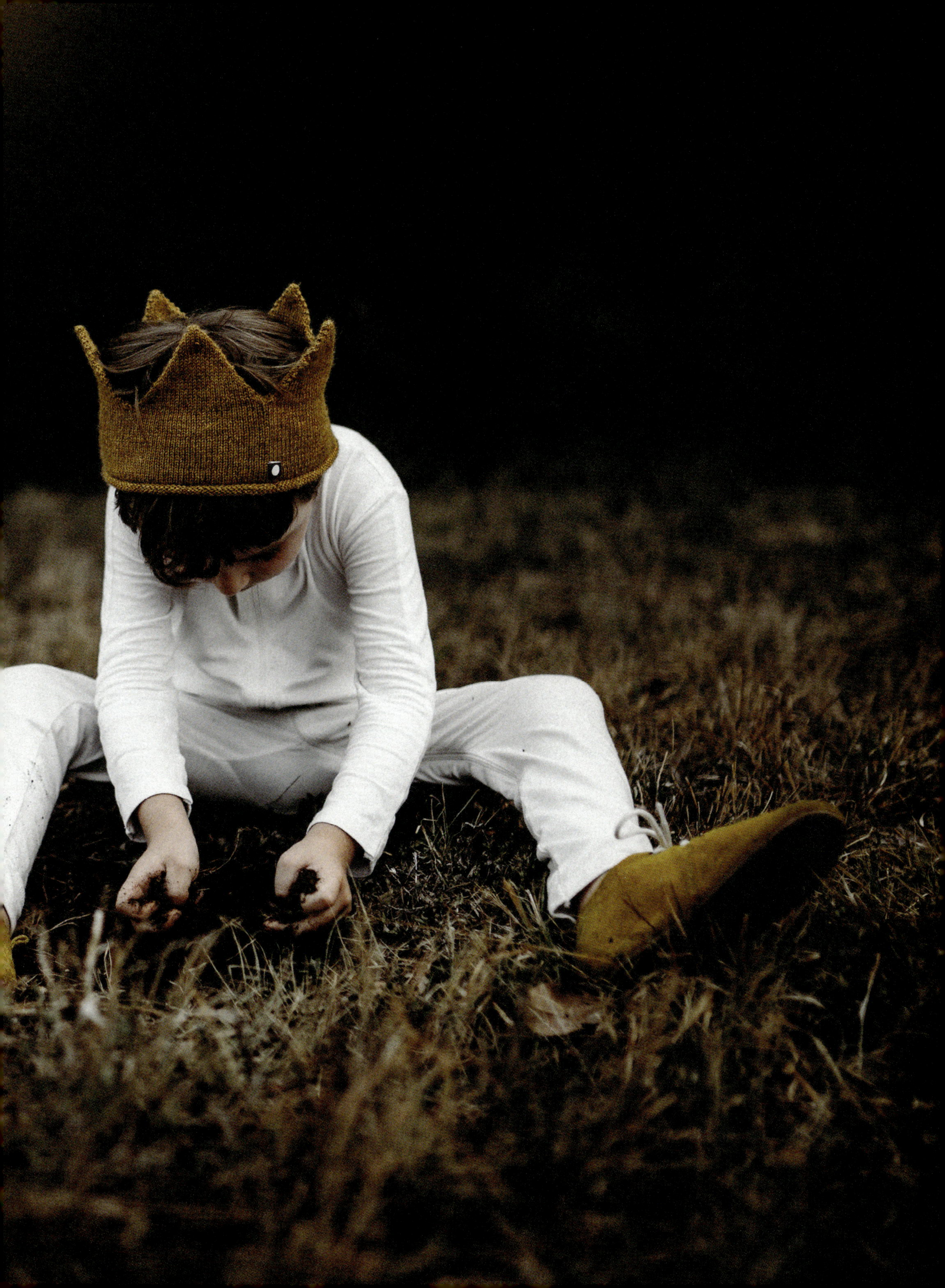

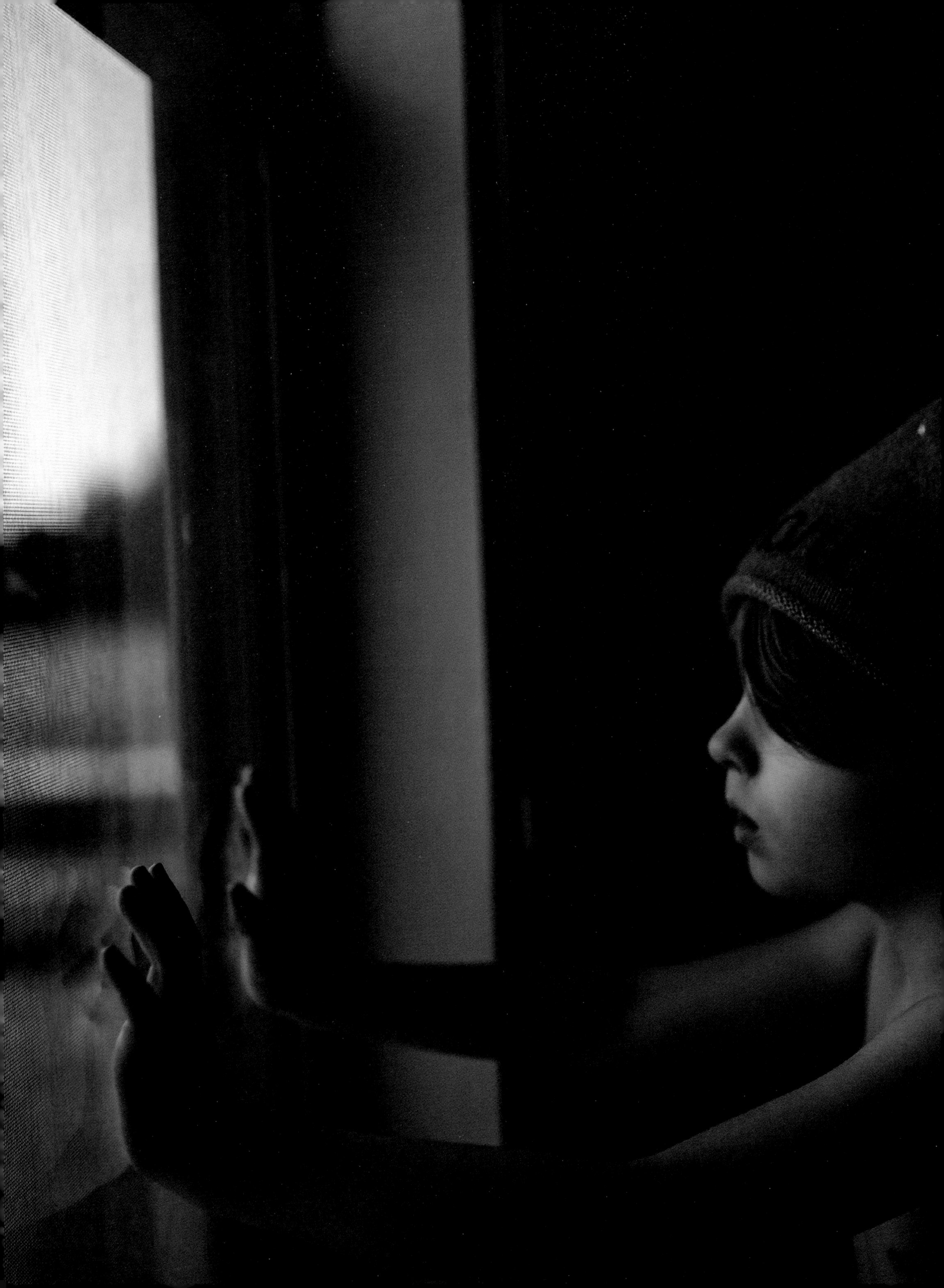

Autism

After weeks of speech and occupational therapy, Charlie wasn't making any progress, he was regressing. The word "autism" kept coming back up in conversations. His therapists weren't qualified to diagnose autism, but they had enough experience working with developmentally delayed children to know when there was more than just a delay causing issues in a child's development. They knew. They knew my son was autistic. But I needed definite answers, so I started doing my own research.

I'm usually against asking "Dr. Google" for advice because I usually end up with self-diagnosed stage 4 lung cancer or something of the type, but the Internet happened to be very useful. I looked up signs and symptoms of autism in babies and toddlers, and my jaw dropped. It was as if the list was tailor-made for Charlie. Was he really autistic? The more I learned about autism, the more convinced I was that Charlie was indeed autistic.

Every time I thought about the possibility of Charlie being on the autism spectrum, the thoughts crashed down on me like a wave knocking me to the ground. It was overwhelming. So instead of focusing on my paralyzing feelings, I pushed forward. Charlie needed an official autism diagnosis which can only be given by a neurologist or developmental pediatrician; that's where my energy had to go.

The waiting lists were long. The initial appointment we booked with the specialist was six months away, an eternity when early intervention means so much. So we called the developmental pediatricians' office again, explaining how desperate we were and told the lady on the phone to call us at any time if there was a cancellation…and it worked. They had just had a cancellation and we could have the appointment at 8:30 AM the following Monday! We'd skipped a six-month waiting list. It was our first victory, and the ball was rolling. We were finally going to be able to get Charlie the help he needed. He didn't have a voice, but as long as I was by his side, he'd always have a friend, mom, and advocate.

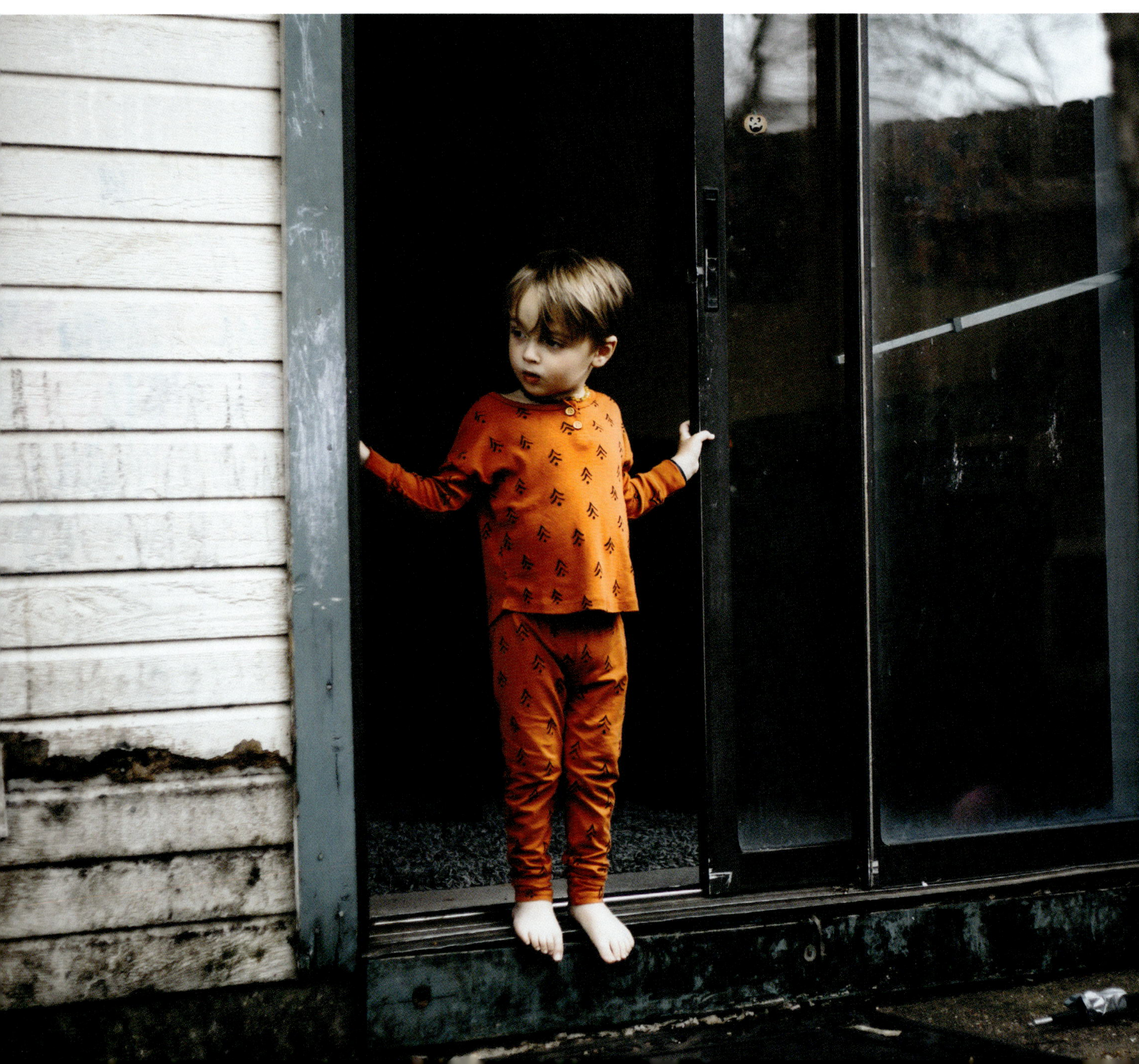

❚ He's autistic. ❚

The big day came fast: Charlie's autism evaluation. A big part of me felt happy to be there and I knew it was the right thing to do, but I was also terrified. I didn't know what to expect. An autism diagnosis would mean a lot more help for Charlie, but it would also mean that our lives would be forever changed.

The developmental pediatrician who entered the room looked serious. Dr. Jones introduced herself to us, but her eyes were on Charlie, observing him, taking him in. "Hi, Charlie," she said, enunciating clearly while crouched in front of him. Charlie didn't even look at her as he pushed a chair across the room.

She observed him with an air of curiosity. Charlie had reached the wall with his chair and positioned it right underneath the light switch, at which point he climbed on top of it and started flicking the switch on and off, giggling the whole time. That was so Charlie. In those 30 seconds, Charlie had given her most of the information she needed. He didn't pay attention to her entering the room, didn't answer to his name, didn't respond to her further attempts at interaction, and displayed what we knew to be a repetitive behavior, the flicking on and off of the light switch. She decided to let him do his own thing for a while and ask us questions. She was going to administer the M-CHAT, but we had brought in a copy of the results. I saw the look on her face when she saw his score of 18. She knew she was going to have to say those words. Words we will never forget. After an hour of crossing the t's and dotting the i's she said, "Charlie's behaviors are consistent with an autism spectrum disorder diagnosis."

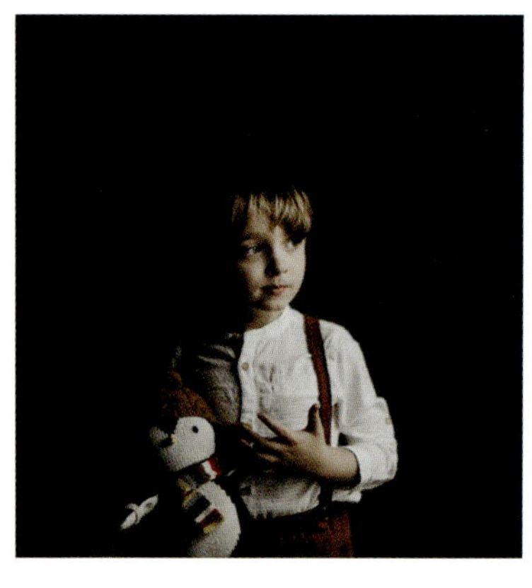

Dr. Jones had no doubt that Charlie was autistic. Because I wanted to be prepared, I had pictured this moment in my mind. I thought I was going to break down in tears, but that didn't happen. I didn't cry. In fact, I felt relief. We finally knew why Charlie was different, and most importantly we were going to be able to get him into more therapy, which he needed.

Dr. Jones recommended that we start with 25 hours of ABA therapy per week and increase his weekly hours as he got older. She handed us a few pamphlets and printed some information about autism from her computer, seven pages of black-and-white text and pictures—information any trained monkey could get online in about 3.1 seconds. But along with it, she handed us the official written diagnosis. That was it. We were on our own now.

My entire world came crashing down, the walls caved in, the floor dropped out from under me, and every other metaphor to that effect. I knew he was autistic and I was prepared to hear the diagnosis, but it hit me hard. I still had so many unanswered questions. Questions no one had the answers to then, and questions I still don't have the answers to now, years later. How severely autistic was Charlie? Will he ever be able to live an independent life? Some autistics are able to communicate. Will Charlie ever have a voice of his own?

Charlie's Autism Signs

	Delayed speech
	Speech regression
	Does not answer to his name
	Does not greet us, his parents, when we come home
Speech	Cannot follow directions
	Ignores other children
	Likes to be alone
	Avoids eye contact
Social Skills	Sometimes gets scared or bothered for no apparent reason and covers his eyes or ears
	Lines up his toys
	Can occupy himself for extended periods of time
	Focuses on details of his toys and misses their broader purpose (just spins the wheel on a car)
	Gets upset by minor changes
	Strange sleep habits (sleeps on floor, etc.)
	Gets frustrated easily
	Has obsessive interests (balls, wheels, light switches)
	Plays with toys the exact same way for long periods of time (i.e., pouring water from one cup to another)
	Likes routines
Unusual Behaviors	Gets "stuck" on things and can't move to other activities
	Hand flapping
	Covers his eyes/ears when bothered by something
	Picky eating
	Sensitive to texture (didn't like walking on the grass, cannot sleep without his silk pillowcase)
Miscellaneous	Throws violent temper tantrums

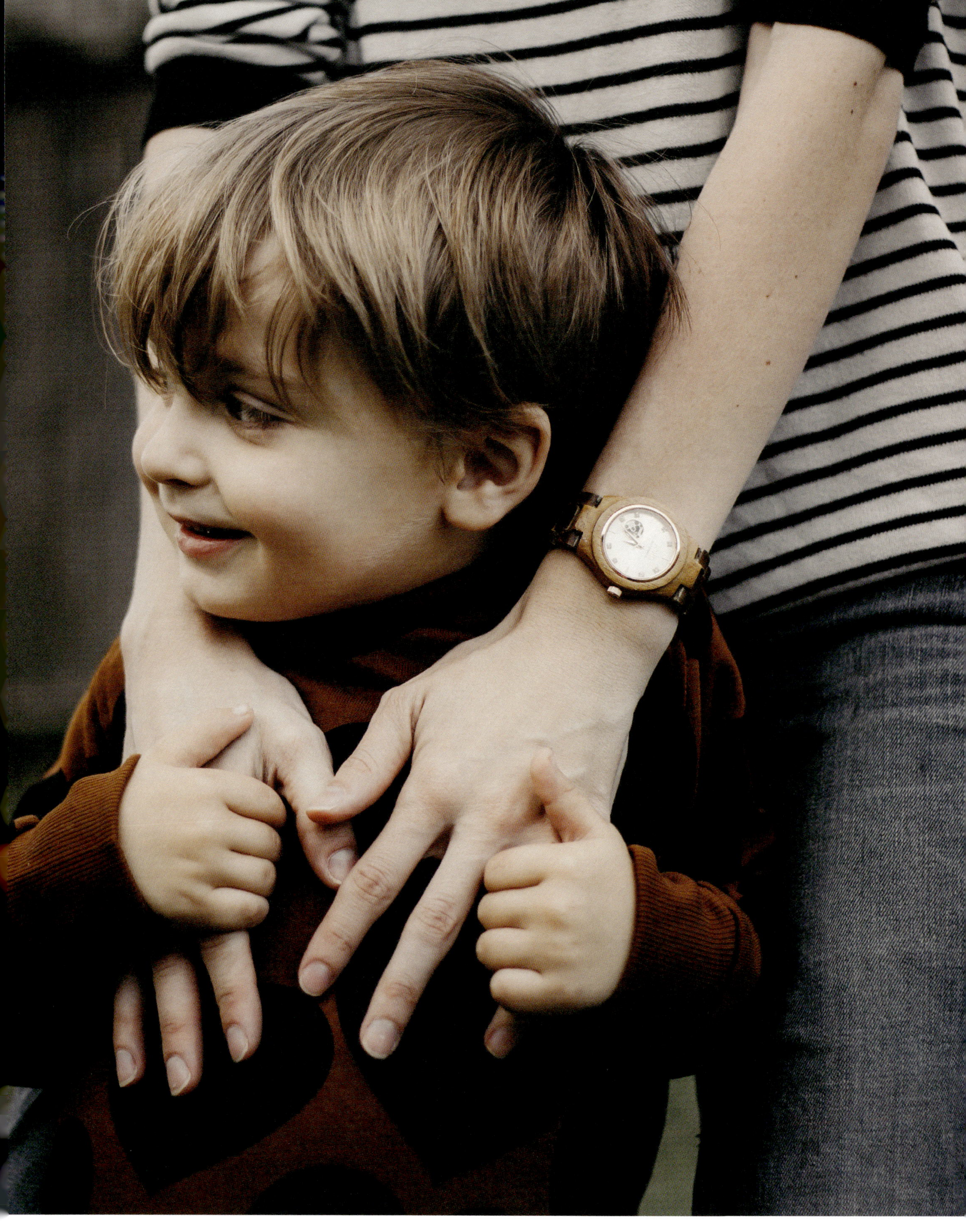

That's such an American thing.

When I need to protect myself from overwhelming emotions, I have a defense mechanism that kicks in. I quickly create a shell around me to block out all negative thoughts and feelings. But as I've learned, the issue with protecting yourself from sad emotions is that you're also preventing yourself from feeling anything. When you build walls around you, they create a fortress: Nothing gets in and nothing gets out. You end up closing yourself off from all the happiness life has to offer.

After Charlie's diagnosis, I was deeply rooted in my own emotional fortress. I just felt numb.

But I had to keep pushing forward for Charlie, so I tried to force myself to focus on the positives: My son was physically healthy. He also had an amazing chance to get an early diagnosis with an early start in ABA therapy. ABA therapy…I couldn't believe how much controversy there was around it. I began to discover a world I had no idea existed, and there was a lot of fiery disagreement in this new world. Professionals recommended Applied Behavior Analysis Therapy (ABA therapy), but some people wrote about it like it was torture! Willy and I decided to trust the experts, and so began our new life. A new life at home that became punctuated with constant therapy and doctors' appointments.

Charlie got used to his new schedule pretty quickly: 25 hours of ABA therapy a week. I was happy to see him getting the help he needed, but I needed a sanctuary of my own. So I turned to social media. I thought it might help me disconnect from our new reality, but it was becoming painful. It was difficult for me to see my Facebook friends' posts showing how well their children were doing. They'd share pictures and videos of them saying funny things and mispronouncing words, and I just wished I had that, too. Of course, I was happy for them, but behind my smile and my "likes," I was suffering. Alone in my fortress.

When I started telling people I trusted about Charlie's autism diagnosis, no one wanted to believe it. I kept getting the same responses: "He'll be fine," "My kid does that, too," "He just needs more time," "Autism is overdiagnosed," "He's so young, there's no way to know," and, from my parents in France, "That's such an American thing." I thought to myself, "and your reaction is very French."

There's a stigma about disability and mental health in France. I remember hiding when going to my therapist as a young adult for fear of being mocked. I'd put the hood of my sweatshirt up whenever I entered the building. The French believe that only "crazy" people need to see a therapist. You can imagine how insane the idea of having a 2-year-old in therapy for 25 hours a week sounded to the Frenchies in my life. But when I heard my mom say that autism is "such an American thing," I started thinking. Is it an American thing? It's true that there are more than four times as many diagnosed children with autism in the United States per capita than in France. But it's likely that this means that America has better resources available to diagnose autism. I suppose people were just trying to reassure me by telling me Charlie wasn't actually autistic, but it had the oppo-site effect. I felt alone and misunderstood.

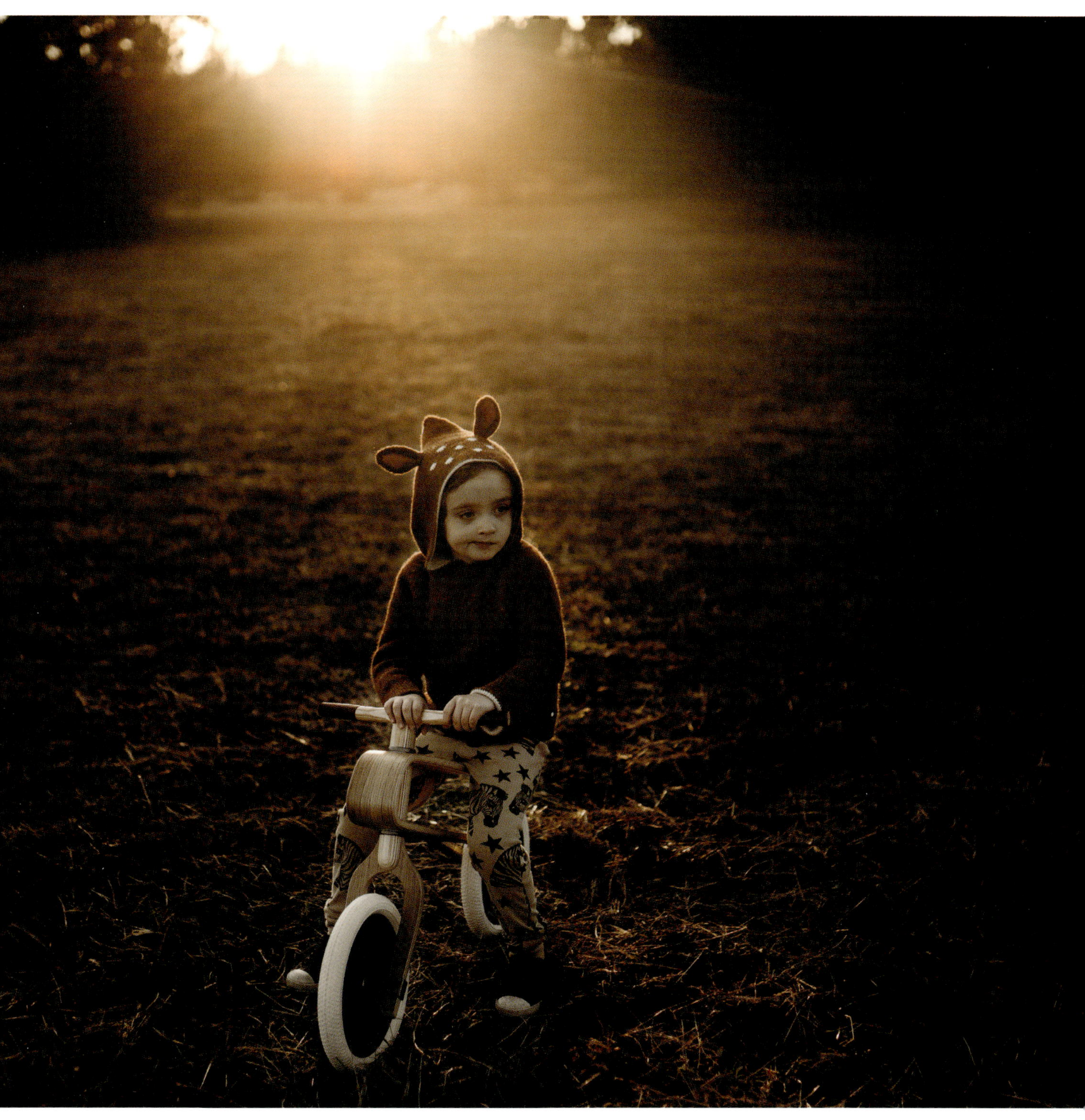

You are not alone.

The months went by and I started to notice my mom friends drifting away from me more and more. I didn't have the time nor the energy to socialize. Charlie was such a handful in public. He didn't follow directions. He ran around uncontrollably. He screamed. None of it was fun; not for me or the people I was with. Still, though, I wish someone had tried to reach out to me, even if it was uncomfortable. I wish someone had stopped by and brought pizza and beer and offered to chat. It was a lonely time. I didn't have anyone in Texas who "got it," someone who knew what it was like to have a life full of therapy, communication devices, and intense tantrums. So I started writing. It was therapeutic. Early on, I wrote this post, not knowing it would eventually become the beginnings of my blog. I wrote this simply because it was what I wanted to hear at that time.

To the mom running her child to ABA therapy while her friends are driving their children to soccer practice, you're not alone.

To the mom carrying around a PECS book, you rock!

To the dad avoiding milestone conversations with his friends because his child is years behind, your child is perfect just the way he is.

To the mom embarrassed by her son's screams at the grocery store, I've been there, too—yesterday, actually.

To the mom on her computer researching what kind of therapy is best for her child, your child is lucky to have you as his advocate.

To the dad afraid of taking his child to a restaurant, park, or any kind of public place, I know—it's difficult.

To the mom still mourning the dream of taking her son to the movies or baseball practice, it may not happen how you pictured it, but it will.

To the dad feeling silly because he celebrated when his son said "buh" for bubbles, every single victory is worth celebrating. Open up that champagne!

To the mom holding in her tears after another therapy report that makes her feel like her child is not progressing, don't lose hope!

To the dad wishing his daughter would talk, me, too—you're not alone.

You are not alone! We are not alone. When you feel hopeless, when you're struggling to keep going, remember that you're not alone. When you feel like nobody notices you unless your child is screaming...when you're wondering how you're going to do it any longer, I want you to remember that you're doing an amazing job. I know you love your child—you're doing the best you can. When you feel like nobody understands what you're going through, remember that I do and there are a lot of us out here.

It's okay to have bad days—we all do. To all the moms and dads out there who are trying their hardest to give their children the best life possible despite the circumstances, you are amazing and your child knows it even if he/she can't say it. Here's to you!

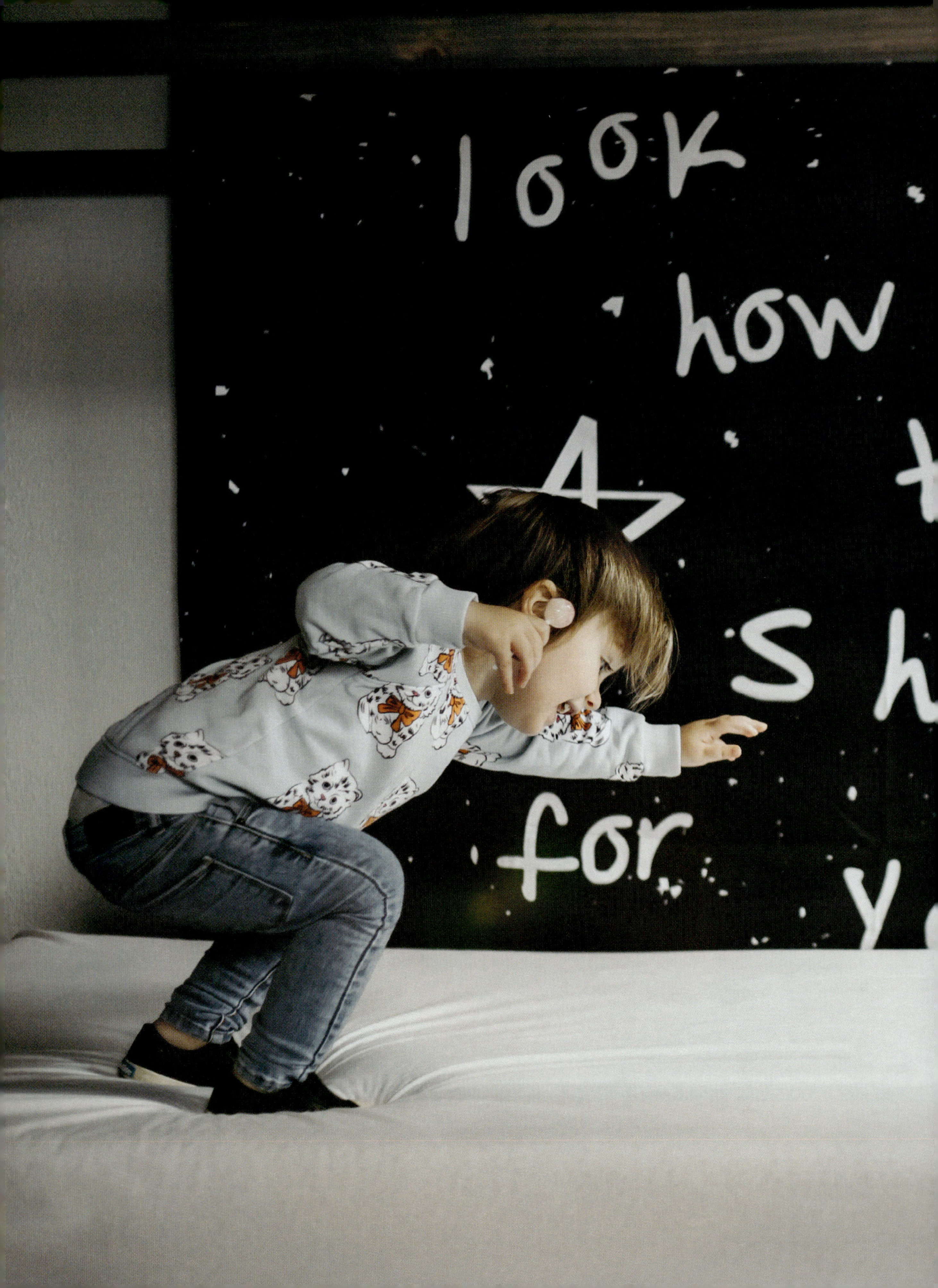

look
how
s
sh
for
y

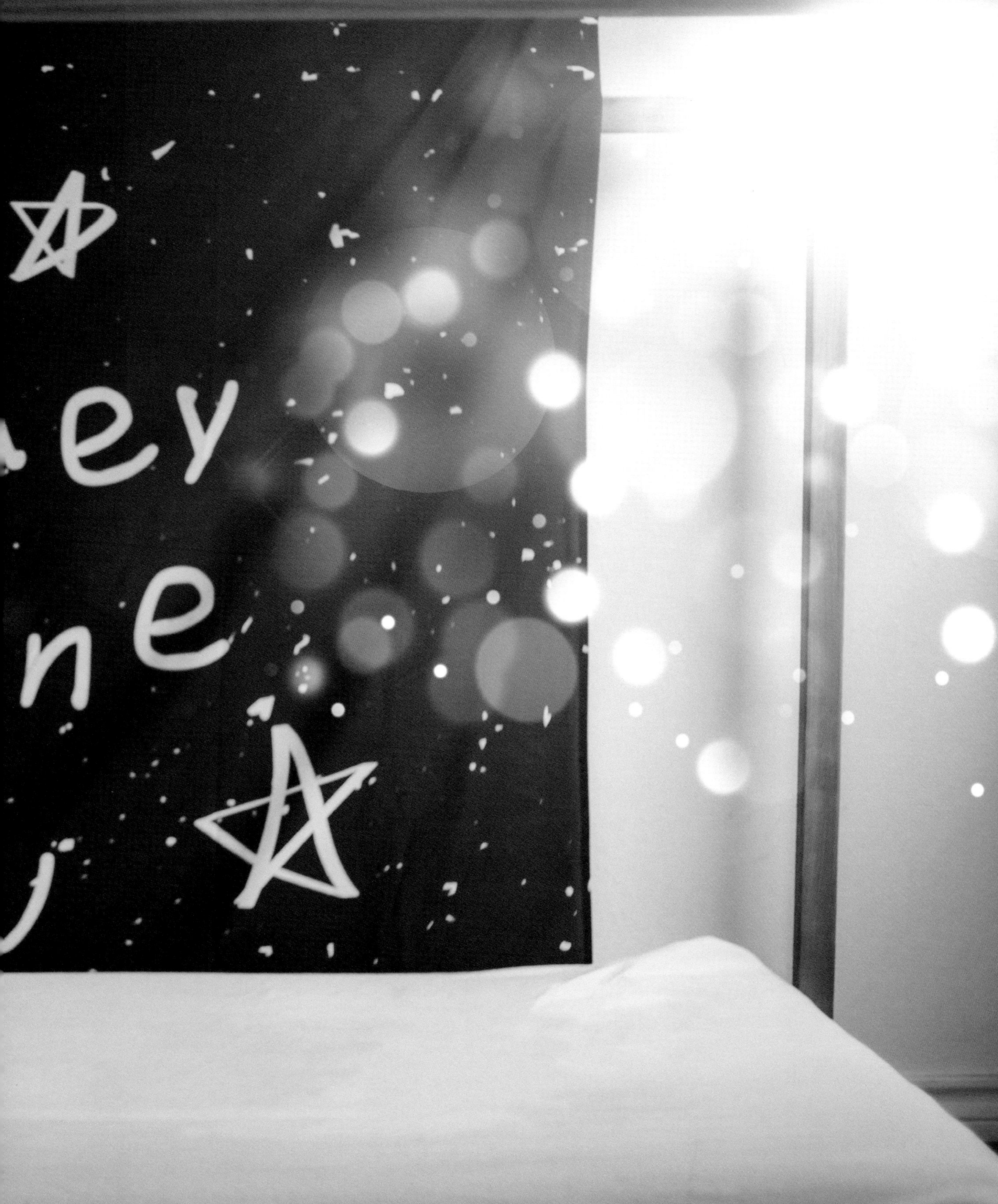

Dr. Robble

After Charlie was diagnosed with autism, it took a few weeks for my mom to finally come around and accept that Charlie's diagnosis wasn't just "an American thing." I was honestly really proud of her for acknowledging this fact; I know it was hard for her. It took her a while to come around because she wasn't so convinced that Charlie couldn't be autistic since I was the exact same way as a child.

The next few months were wrought with this odd, nagging suspicion. My mom's connection between Charlie and myself as a child really shocked me. Her words had put down roots and consumed my thoughts. One day, I was browsing the internet, and an ad popped up: "signs of autism in adults." I got curious and tapped it. My jaw dropped. Just like with Charlie, I felt like the list was tailor-made for me. The site also had an autism screening tool; I took it and it came back as high risk for autism. But I shrugged it off. What could an online quiz know about me? I couldn't be autistic, I thought. I'm…me, and I always have been.

There was such a big difference between me and Charlie. Sure, I was struggling socially and a little bit quirky, but I didn't feel like these traits of mine—parts of me that I'd lived with since as long as I could remember—could be rooted in the same condition affecting Charlie.

At least that's what I said to convince myself because the idea that I could be autistic, too, made my head spin. It didn't compute. What would autism mean for me? It was too much to handle. My mind was like a puzzle trying to connect the pieces, but it wasn't one I could solve on my own. I needed help.

I decided to call an autism specialist in Austin named Dr. Chuck Robble. Willy and I had consulted with her in the past to get her professional expertise on therapies and services that would be best for Charlie. If I was going to have to go through a lengthy assessment to find answers about myself, she seemed like a great choice.

In an attempt to save a little money of the staggering price of the assessment, I agreed to have all the sessions video-recorded so Dr. Robble could use them in training seminars with students. She had no idea when she agreed to do the full therapeutic assessment with me that I was indeed going to be diagnosed with autism after having lived my entire life up to that point without knowing, and that she and I would be making this discovery together. Now, videos of myself during this assessment are being used to teach students about signs of autism in adults.

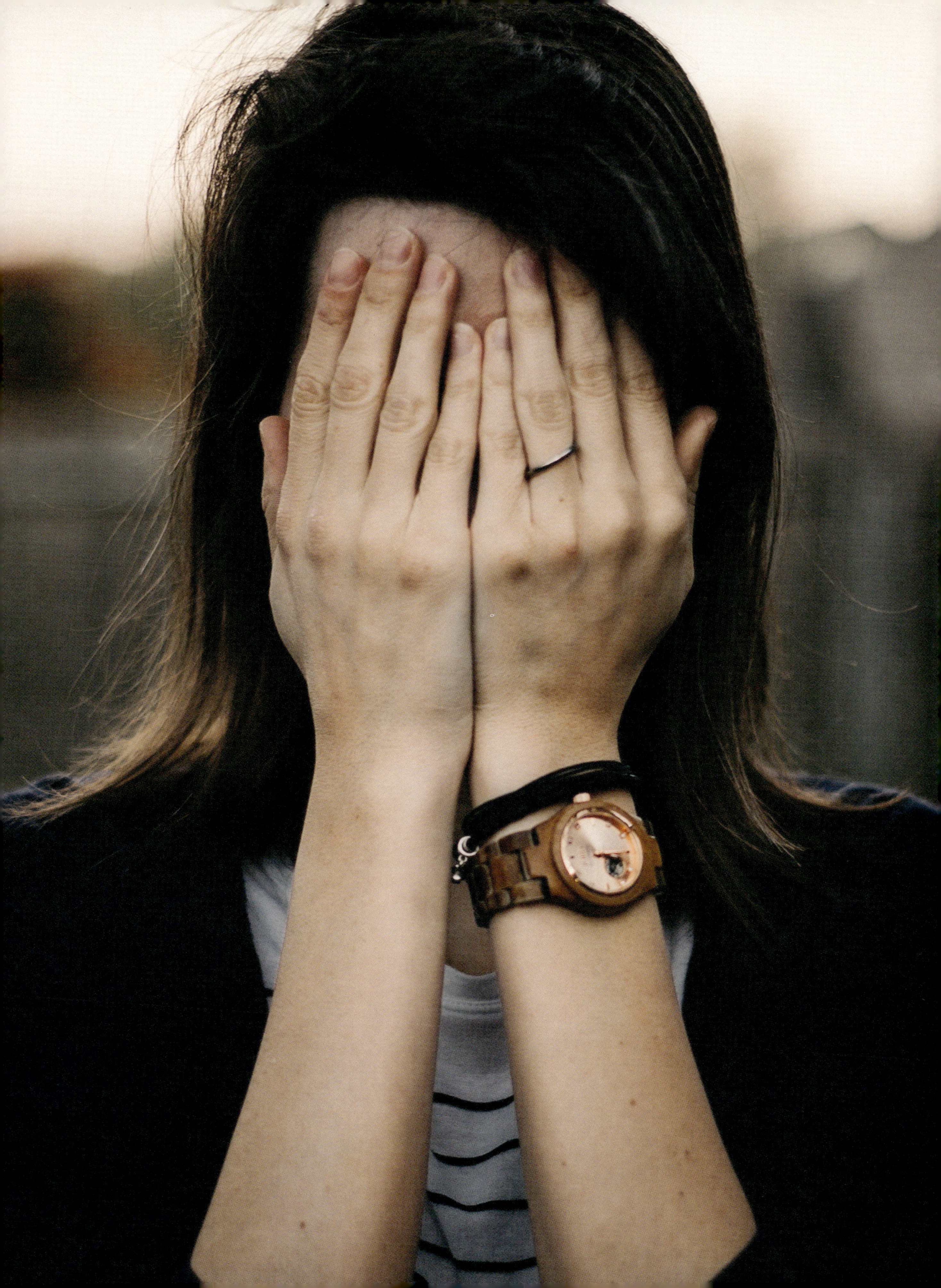

A crispy baguette, please and thank you.

Sitting in the reception room waiting for Dr. Robble to call me in, I started to feel nervous. I couldn't sit still and kept wiggling around as if my chair was on fire. I had been seeking answers about myself for as long as I could remember. These appointments had life-changing potential. I was really hoping to find some answers. And that was the therapist's first question: "What are you expecting to get from this assessment?"

I wanted to know why I had always felt different, why all my friendships were failing one way or another. Why couldn't I do simple things like going to the store to buy a gallon of milk without feeling wiped out? Why did I feel so misunderstood? Why were social interactions so complicated for me? Why was it so difficult for me to connect with people emotionally? Why did I feel so out of place in this world? Was I autistic?

And the assessment started. I spent hours sitting in Dr. Robble's office answering questions, filling out questionnaires, and doing cognitive testing. As I was filling out one of the surveys, a question stopped me in my tracks. It was about my ability to adapt in unknown situations. I smiled, thinking that this definitely isn't one of my strengths. My lack of common sense and adaptability have put me in awkward situations more times than I can count.

In France, we have an abundance of independent bakeries and butchers. They look like little boutiques and oftentimes the butcher and the bakery are right next door. There are many clichés about the French that aren't necessarily true, but there's one that holds up: We can basically survive on baguettes.

One day when I was ten my mom needed a baguette for dinner, so she pulled up to the storefront and told me to repeat these words: "a crispy baguette, please and thank you." She knew I hated communicating with strangers like this, but it was her way of trying to teach me important social skills. Because I would often freeze up when talking to people, she'd always coach me on what to say beforehand.

Usually, bakeries had an outdoor glass display showcasing colorful macarons and other delicious French pastries. This store didn't. When I entered the store, all I could see was meat. The guy behind the counter was wearing a white suit and gloves covered in blood. I stood there puzzled until he asked, "Can I help you?" I repeated word-for-word what my mom instructed me to say. "A crispy baguette, please and thank you."

The guy stared at me for a second. I think he was waiting for a "just kidding," but I didn't say it. I wasn't. I was serious. My mom needed that crispy baguette, and I was going to get it.

After what felt like an eternity he burst out laughing, pointed to the store next door, and said, "The bakery is next door, petite."

I slowly walked out of the store towards my mom, who was inside the car crying real tears of laughter. She asked if I had really just asked the butcher for a crispy baguette. I nodded. At the time, I felt confused and a little bit betrayed. Maybe the meat should have given it away, but my mom had parked right in front of the butcher and pointed to that store.

As I've learned, common sense still isn't my strong suit. A few months ago, I tried washing my cardboard sewing box in the washing machine. Needless to say, that didn't end well for the box nor the washing machine.

Do you obsess over things?

The sessions went by and I kept filling out questionnaires and answering Dr. Robble's questions. Another survey, another question. And more memories would come flooding back. The next item on the survey asked about my tendency to obsess over things and if it was true "now," "before," or "now and then." The answer to this question was undeniably yes, at least "now and then."

I remember, even at a young age, my deep desire to learn about certain topics caused me a great deal of anxiety. Volcanoes, planets, asteroids, UFOs. I thought about these topics so much and with such intensity that it was hard to focus on anything else. There was just so much mystery around them. I can see myself as a young child, sitting at the library trying to find information about volcanoes. Upstairs there was a tiny room I loved with an area covered with pillows. I've always felt comforted in small, confined spaces. I'd often hide in my bedroom closet to daydream. It was soothing; I felt protected and safe as if the world was hugging me.

At the library, I would search for books with information about volcanoes. I wanted to know how far the closest volcano was to my city, Troyes. I was trying to prepare myself in case of a volcanic eruption. I needed to know if lava could reach us, and if so, how quickly and in which direction we needed to drive to escape. Logically, the probability of this happening was close to zero, but still, I felt the need to obsessively prepare.

Through the years, my anxiety and fixations didn't improve. I developed a new fear and obsession every month, and it would only go away when I had learned everything I could about the subject. My parents were aware of my anxiety and obsessions, but they never took me to see a therapist. I only saw my first therapist as a young adult after I started making money on my own playing poker. I'm not mad at my parents for not getting me help. It's just how they were raised. It's what they've learned was normal. Anxiety, depression—in most French people's minds, mental health is something only the weak are affected by. For the rest, you just deal with it, shut up, and try to feel better. My anxiety, though, was real and paralyzing. Dr. Robble later explained to me that the intensity with which I dive in when I'm interested in something isn't typical and is part of my autism diagnosis.

You have high-functioning autism.

Each day provided more and more assessments. I would sit in Dr. Robble's office and become completely distracted by the hundreds of books and interesting objects. Thirteen birds and owls lined the shelves. I wondered why she liked birds so much. Did she, too, have obsessions? The street was loud and disruptive, but even in the privacy of her office, I was careful not to show signs of discomfort when disturbed by a noise. It's a social behavior I've learned to control in order to fit in better.

Finally, after two weeks of testing, she said it: "Eileen, you have high-functioning autism." Boom. I felt a whole range of emotions, from relief to anxiety and everything in between. The moment was hard to describe. I was different. I knew it. But along with some relief, I also felt guilty. Was Charlie autistic because of me?

When I got into my car, the anxiety hit me like a brick. How was the official diagnosis going to affect my life? What were people going to think of me now? The uncertainty put me into a tailspin. It was scary as if I was driving on a dark road, unable to see what was awaiting me at the next turn. I quickly went back into my fortress to protect myself from all of these emotions bombarding me at once.

Dr. Robble wrote a long letter to me, which is part of the therapeutic assessment process, explaining why she diagnosed me with autism. It provided me with so many answers. Answers I had always wanted. What struck me in her letter is that unbeknownst to me, even as we talked at that first session, she thought I might indeed be autistic. According to her, I reported my struggles with little emotion or facial expression. My eye contact was fleeting, and at times I was distracted by sounds that many people might have been able to ignore.

She also noticed me rocking back and forth as I was waiting for her to escort me in the waiting room. Additionally, the results of all the tests and questionnaires I took indicated a high risk for autism. In making her diagnosis, Dr. Robble also talked to people in my life, people who knew me well, like my mom and Willy. They, too, filled out questionnaires and answered questions about me which confirmed Dr. Robble's suspicions that I was indeed autistic. As the therapist kept explaining what part of my personality traits were consistent with an autism diagnosis, I felt like the puzzle in my mind was finally being solved—the pieces were falling into place.

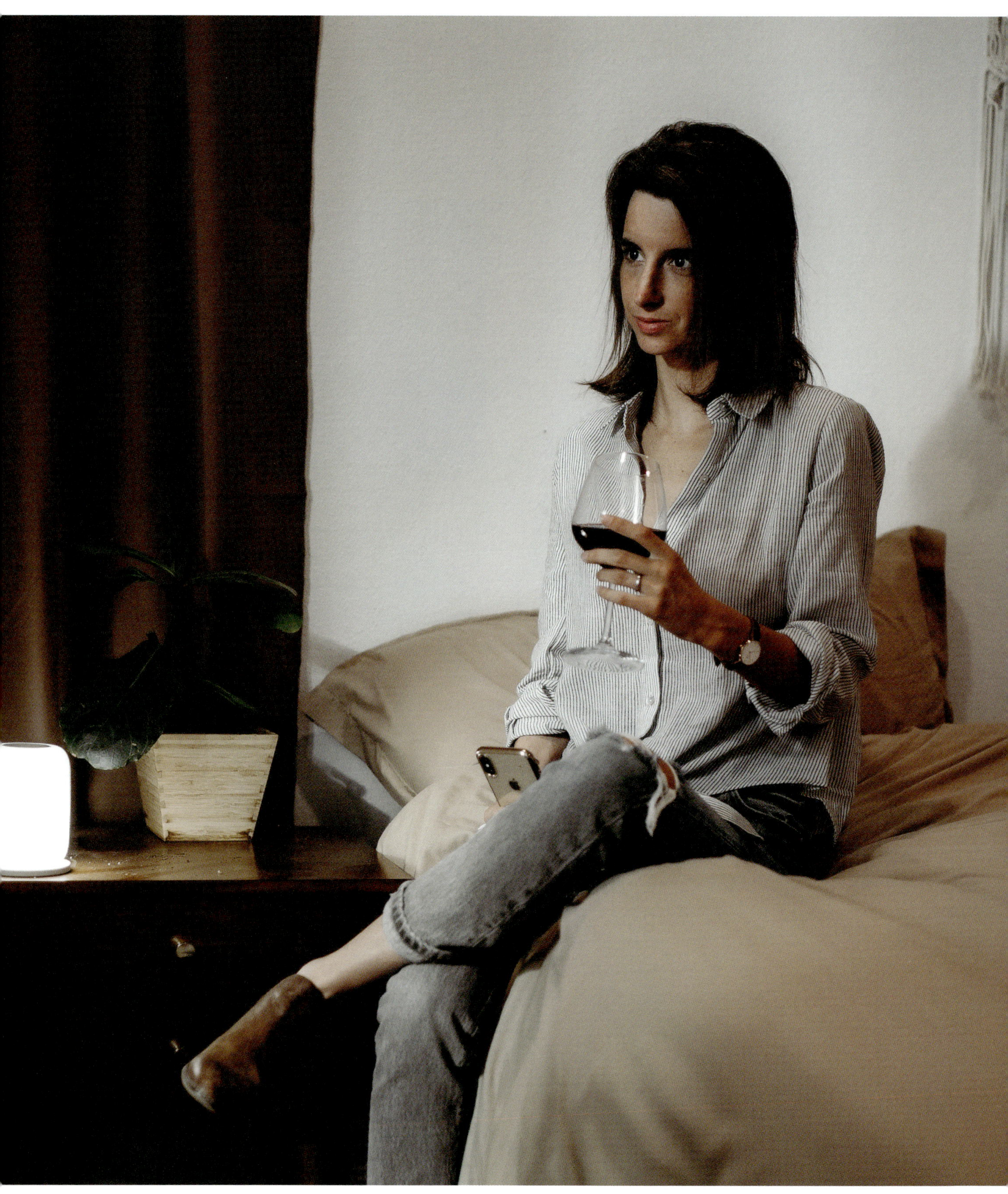

#ActuallyAutistic

Dr. Robble emphasized that I was high-functioning and that I have what was previously defined as Asperger's syndrome, before the changes in the Diagnostic and Statistical Manual of Mental Disorders, Fifth Edition (DSM-5). I like the term Asperger's because to me, it shows the difference between someone like me, who struggles but can mimic social behavior and live an independent life, and someone like Charlie, who is severely autistic and not able to communicate at all. I quickly learned, though, that my need to call myself high-functioning autistic rather than just autistic is really frowned upon among other autistic adults. And that's when the bullying started again.

Social media is a double-edged sword. It can be a beautiful place to form connections, but it can also make your insecurities worse when all you're seeing are other people's highlight reels. I struggled to relate to other moms. It was painful for me to see the developmental gap between Charlie and his peers getting bigger, month after month. Meanwhile, I saw moms on social media complaining that their children were talking too much and that they were sick of hearing "mama" ten times an hour. These posts were devastating because I had been longing to hear Charlie call me 'mommy." They had what I had always wanted.

If autism has taught one important thing, it's not to take things for granted.

We now celebrate even the smallest of milestones, those that may seem meaningless to most people.

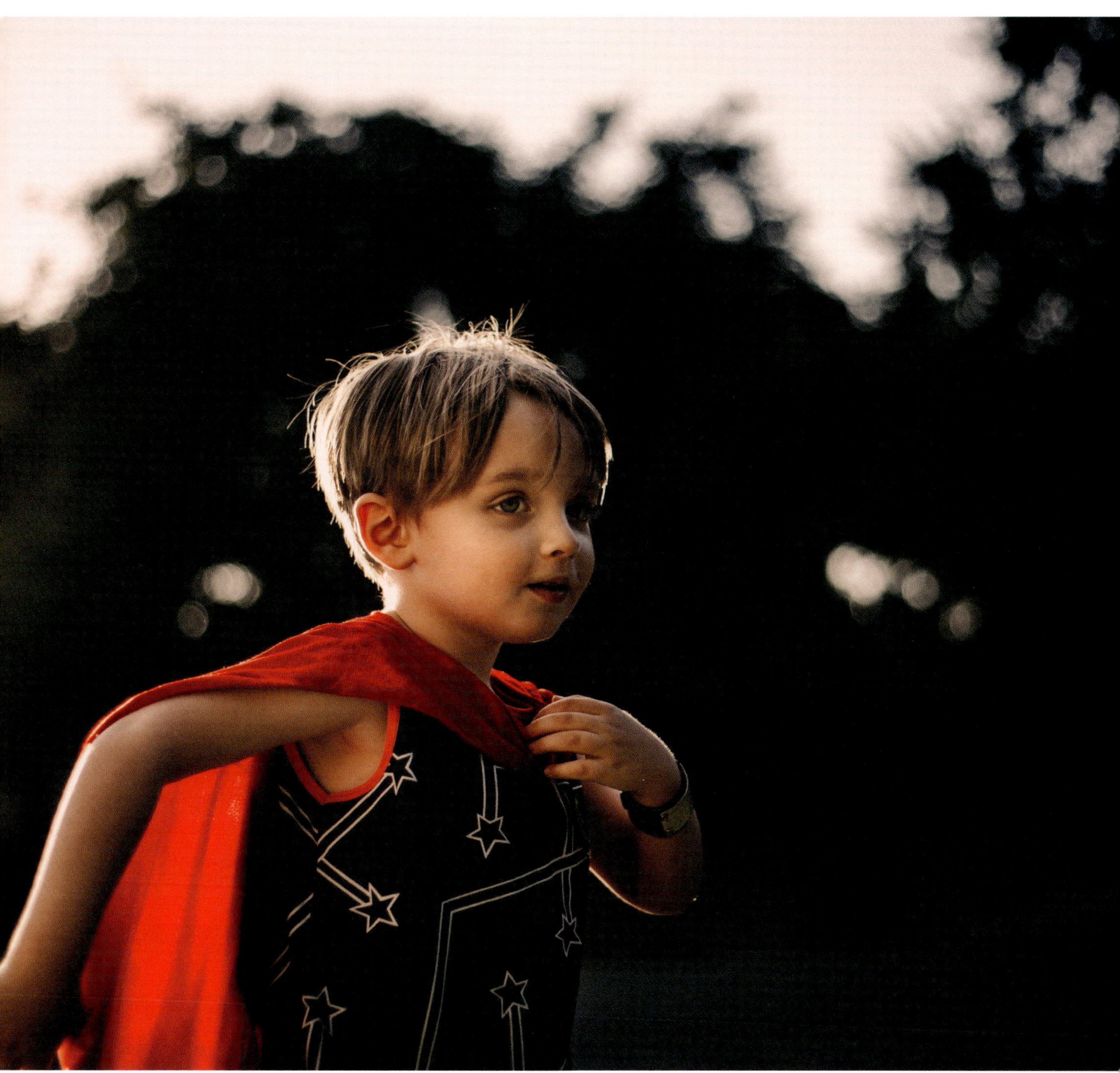

I remember when my youngest son, Jude, clapped his hands for the first time. With tear-filled eyes, Willy and I cheered so loudly that we scared him and he burst into tears.

In an attempt to connect with other parents of autistic children, I started sharing snippets of our life on my blog. The positive responses from other autism parents were overwhelming. I felt happy to be helping people. Writing about autism and our life with Charlie was therapeutic for me, but it also helped others feel like they were not alone. The connections were brief, often just one exchange of emails, but that's all it took to provide me and my readers with a sense of comfort, a glimmer of hope that everything was going to be okay even when life was different from what we expected.

Sadly, with the increase of traffic to my blog, I also got a taste of how audacious and unfiltered people can become when hidden behind their computer screens. The first time I was attacked on my blog, I felt angry but also confused and sad. The people attacking me were also autistic. They call themselves #ActuallyAutistic because they are actually autistic, as opposed to parents of autistic children who often talk about autism from their neurotypical perspective. They believe that autism should only be discussed by autistic people because they are the ones living with it. From their perspective, a neurotypical person cannot understand what an autistic person experiences and so they shouldn't talk about it. They don't want other people to represent them when they are fully able to represent themselves. What they're not taking into consideration is that not all autistics are able to express themselves. Charlie can't.

When your child gets diagnosed with autism, your entire universe shifts. It's lonely. Connecting with people who are living similar experiences has been so helpful to me and other parents that I can't understand why someone would want to prevent that. They would come en masse to my blog, Facebook, and Instagram pages, cyber-bullying me by leaving vicious comments in their wake. Their attacks increased in frequency so that it was happening every time I posted something new.

Finally, I came out as autistic. I naively thought that they would leave me alone after knowing I was one of them. I was wrong. They clung to their labels and shunned me from the community I thought might finally accept me. When the attacks continued with more intensity I considered abandoning my blog, but instead, I found the strength to keep writing for all the people out there who are too afraid to talk about autism because of the #ActuallyAutistic community.

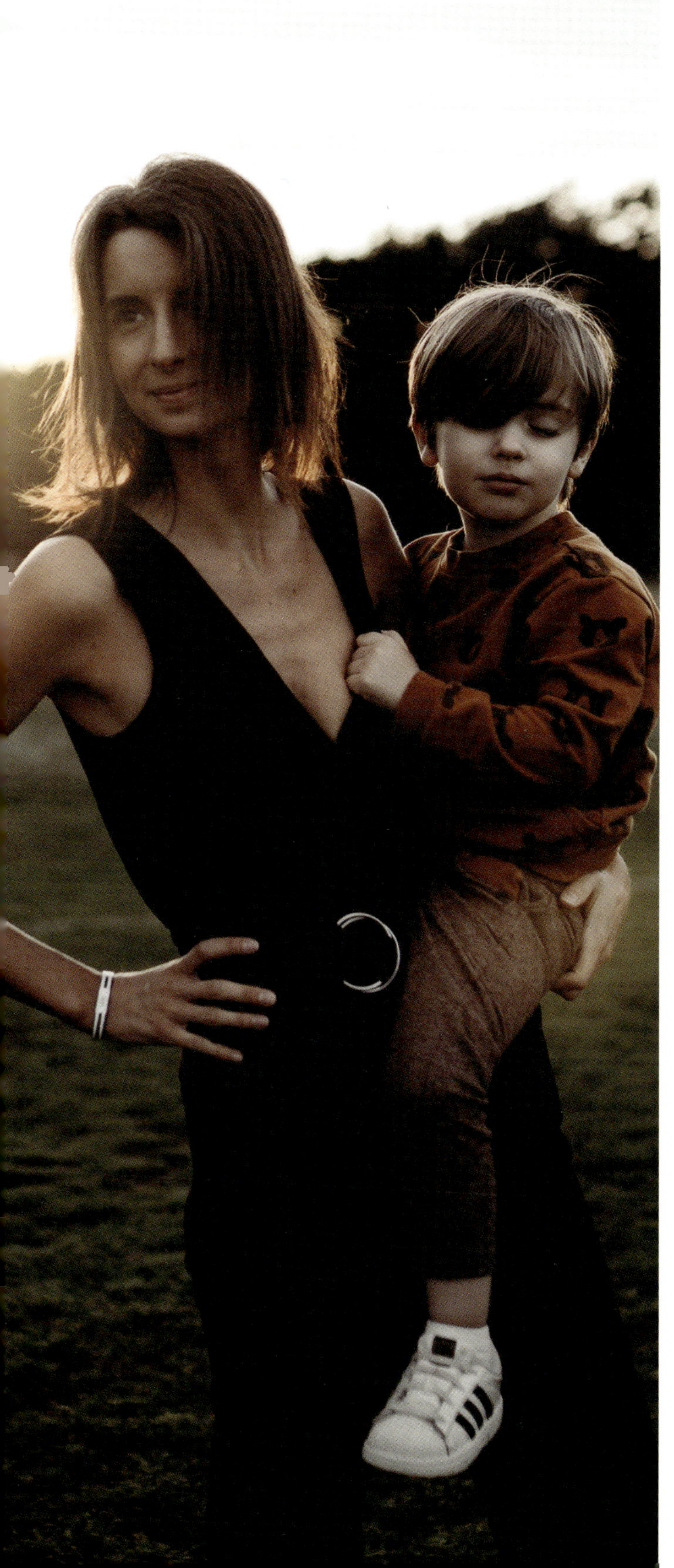

Honesty

My friendships always seem to wither, no matter how hard I try. I can't help but wonder why life keeps throwing people at me who are not meant to stay. I wonder if it's even worth investing in relationships if they're all meant to expire. Is the temporary happiness worth the pain? Shouldn't we walk away before we inevitably suffer? Or maybe relationships just aren't meant to last. Maybe there's beauty in the momentary nature of it. Maybe life puts people in our path simply for the lessons they teach us and inspire us to change, to better ourselves, and to not commit the same mistakes again.

When I meet someone with whom I think I'll get along and it doesn't work out, I really dig into the self-blame. Dr. Robble encourages me to remember that difficulty sustaining friendships is part of my autism diagnosis. Since I started blogging, I've met many people on social media. Some of them were even local to me, turning into real friendships that had us hanging out every week. Just like my other relationships, though, they didn't stand the test of time.

The biggest obstacle to my sustaining a friendship is that I expect full transparency from the people I interact with, and it's difficult for some people to give it. I can't connect with people who aren't completely honest with me. The people with whom I form the most meaningful relationships are the ones who have that capacity for openness. They celebrate my successes, but they also right me when I'm wrong. They're the ones who give me tough love when needed, gently redirecting me if I'm headed off course. I so appreciate this in people because it provides me with a sense of safety because what you see is what you get—there's no need for me to read between the lines, and I know we'll be able to talk things through if a problem arises. It's the grey areas and subtleties in people that I just can't seem to wrap my head around.

I don't get surprised when a relationship ends anymore; that's the pattern. I expect it. I know it's coming. Yet, I see people all around me sharing photos with their friends, and I wish I had that, too. After another failed friendship, I turned my pain into words and started writing. Sometimes we just need to hear that we're not alone, and that can be enough to ease the pain. On Instagram, I shared:

When you're worried that too many betrayals will turn you into a bitter person, remember that there's always a lesson to be learned from each failed relationship. Don't let these failures convince you that you're better off alone. Don't let them convince you that having an open heart is wrong.

When you're worried that there aren't enough people out there who still value honesty, remember that although not everyone appreciates the beauty in people who wear their hearts on their sleeves, some do. You just have to find them.

When you're worried that the whispers and gossip are going to break your fragile heart, remember that every time you thought you couldn't get through a hard time, you always did, and you always will.

The comments on the posts where I open up are usually uplifting and a great reminder that maybe I just haven't met the right friends yet. Some people seem to be open to talking about feelings and raw emotions. And actually, even though I've been struggling a lot in my relationships, there is one friendship in my life that I really hold dear. Funny enough, it began as a professional one and has transformed into something much more. It's an honest relationship that gives me an ongoing reminder that there are amazing people out there who I can connect with, and I just need to find them.

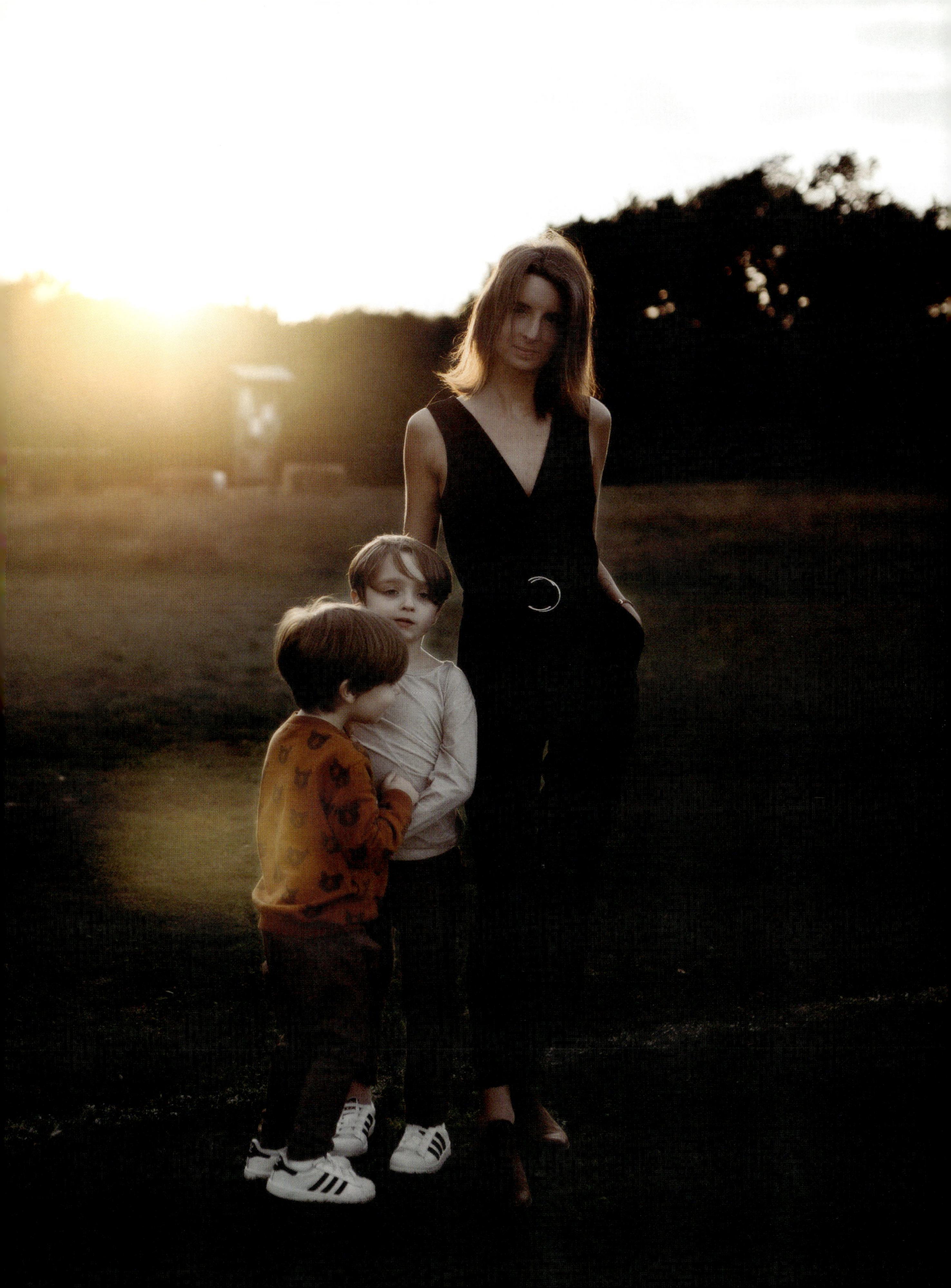

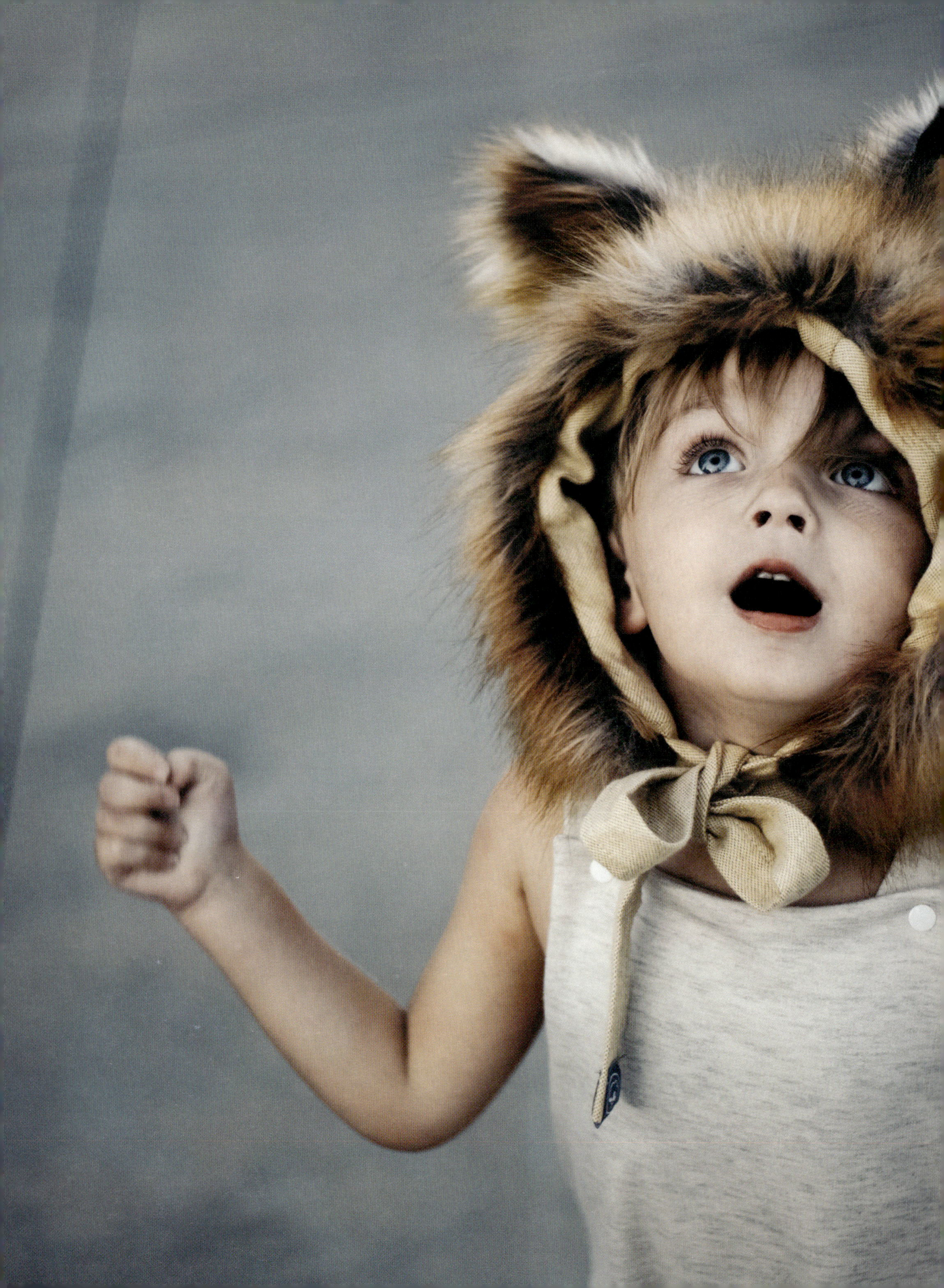

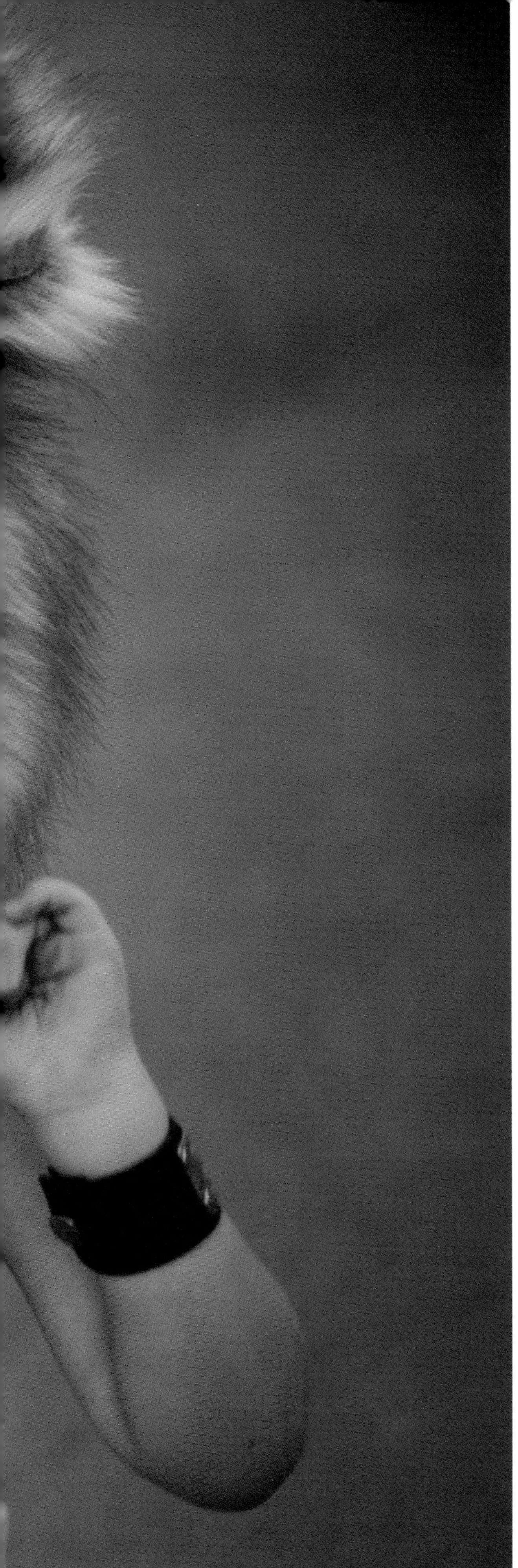

When I tell people I'm autistic, as with many high-functioning individuals, the response I usually get is, "You don't look autistic." I also hear the other side of it from old friends, like, "Ah, that's why you were always doing those stupid things back then (insert awkward laugh)," or, "I knew something was different about you." I get it, it's confusing for people who haven't noticed and it's awkward for those who have. I want to fit in and look neurotypical. Yet when people tell me I don't look autistic, it feels dismissive as if they assume that my autism is not severe enough to matter because my struggles aren't visible. I want to "pass," but I also want people to know what I'm struggling with. I want both.

I wonder what people expect autistic individuals to look like. Autism is a neurological condition that doesn't affect looks. It's probably that they expect all autistic people to act in an obviously awkward or socially oblivious way. For instance, the eponymous character in *Rain Man* is the popular character most associated with autism. The toothpick scene is, in most minds, the quintessential autistic moment. In this

77

scene, the younger brother, Tom Cruise, has rescued Rain Man from a residential center. They're in a bar when the waitress drops a box of toothpicks on the floor. *Rain Man* looks at the toothpicks for a few seconds and correctly counts 246 of them. It's true that a very small percentage of autistic people will be a savant with this kind of "splinter skill," but they make up close to zero percent of autistic individuals.

I'm happy when autism is represented in movies, because it's great to have people talking about it. Since the spectrum is so broad, it would be impossible to please everyone with a realistic representation of autism. I only wish that people watching wouldn't hold on to just one representation.

I can't look at toothpicks on the floor and instantly know how many there are. I'm not a math genius. I don't carry a notepad in my pocket with all the social rules I've learned so I can correct people when they're wrong. And I don't talk about trains all day long. Autism is not as entertaining as it's portrayed in movies, and while my disability is invisible to all but those close to me, it affects my life daily.

I want people to acknowledge that a lot of work goes into me looking "normal" and trying to fit in. I'm glad the work has paid off and that I often "pass," but when people say, "You don't look autistic," it's not really a compliment. And when they don't take full account of my autism, people expect me to behave like everyone else: to make eye contact, chit-chat with the cashier, be able to stay calm and happy during loud noises, to not flap my hands, to not be too blunt, and to be able to understand social cues.

Through the years, I've spent a lot of time trying to blend in, learning tips and tricks to fit in. But sometimes, despite my best effort, I can't. Going grocery shopping, for instance, can be quite the challenge. I always have to give myself a pep talk before making the big decision to head to the store. I wonder if neurotypical people notice how many annoying, intrusive noises there are in a grocery store. Carts rattling on the floor, the chatter of people, children running around, the speakers in the ceiling playing music, people bumping into things, and that one person nearby who's always rearranging a damn bag of chips in their cart, crackling away. Maybe the worst to me is the incessant "bip bip bip" of the cash registers in the background. Because the bips aren't predictable and don't follow a pattern, they drive me crazy. While I'm trying to tune sounds out and not cross people's gazes, I inevitably start bumping into people or things, which causes further discomfort. To me, it seems like a superpower that other people can effortlessly tune things out without feeling overwhelmed. I envy them.

The advantage of having a visible disability is that people see your needs right away and can accommodate.

My invisible disability is something others either don't see or put out of mind when we are together, and if I can't control it, people look at me like I'm from another planet. When I get startled by a noise, I may drop what's in my hands to cover my ears or start flapping my hands. I want people to be kind if that happens, laugh about it with me, but don't act like I'm an alien. Even if you can't see my autism at all times, I'm always autistic and always will be.

Autism is complicated, but I don't want anyone to walk on eggshells around me because they're afraid to say or do something wrong. I'm thankful when people actually take the time to ask questions and show an interest in Charlie, me, or autism in general. I don't want anyone to stay quiet for fear of offending me. I don't want anyone to feel as hesitant as I do. Because there are so many controversies surrounding autism, it's still sometimes difficult for me to muster the courage to talk about it. Even with my blog. I live in fear of saying the wrong thing and incurring the wrath of those angry individuals who feel strongly about their views. But we have to keep talking about autism. Many of us autistic adults are happy to engage in discussions. Here are some conversation openers: "What is it like for you?" "What can I do to help you?" or "Can I ask you questions?" As much as I cringe when people tell me I don't look autistic, I still appreciate people making an effort to talk about it.

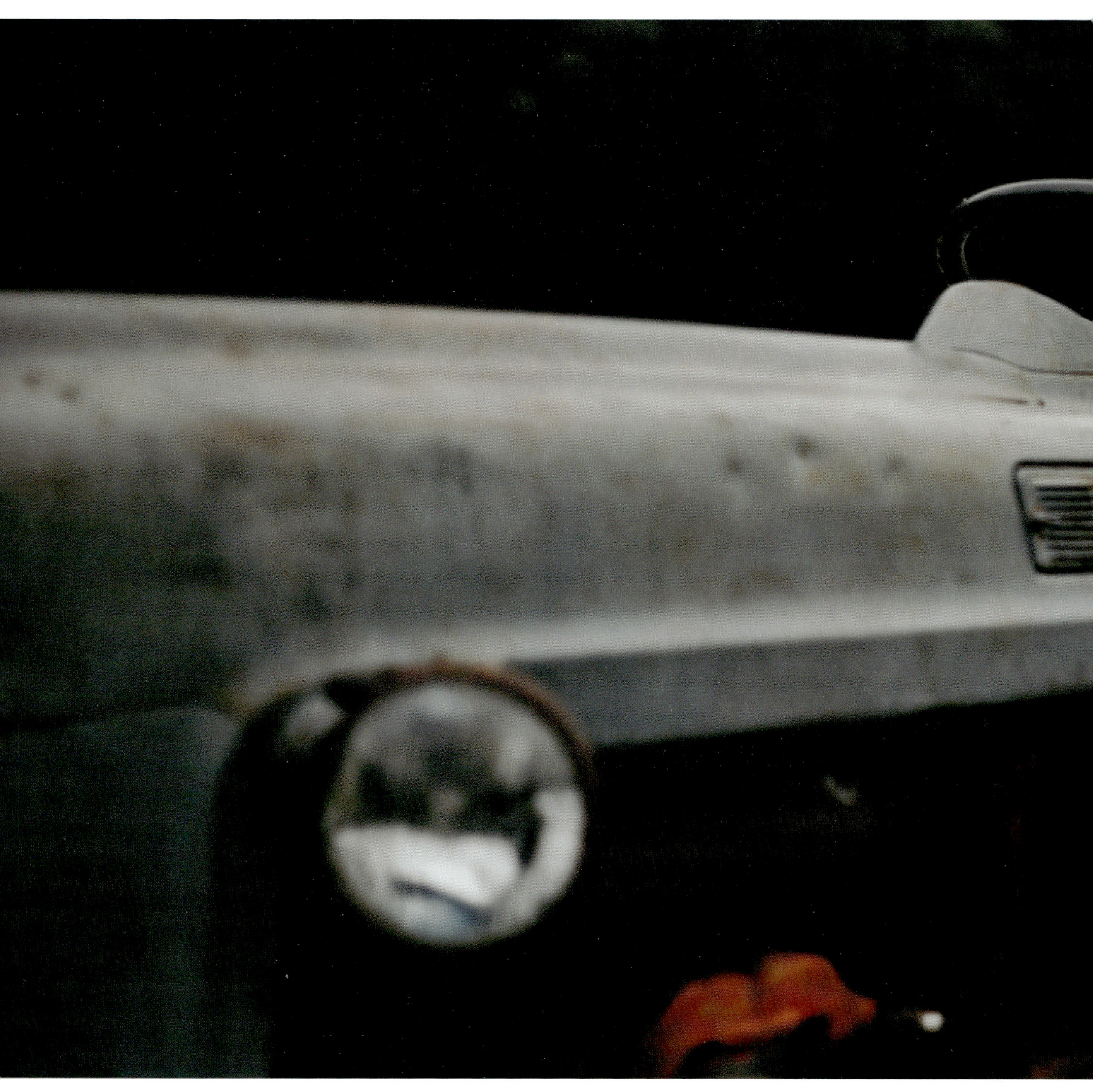

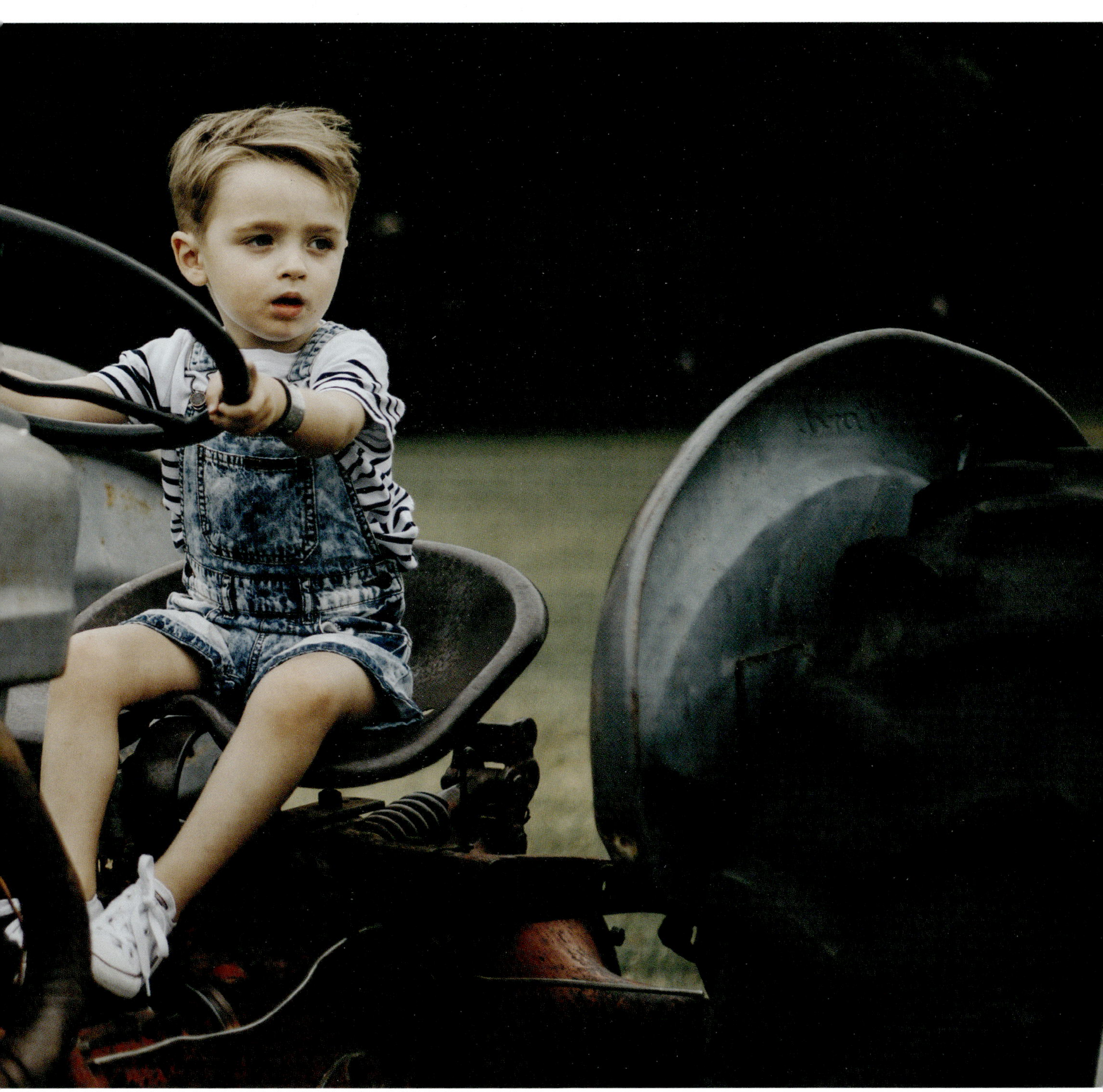

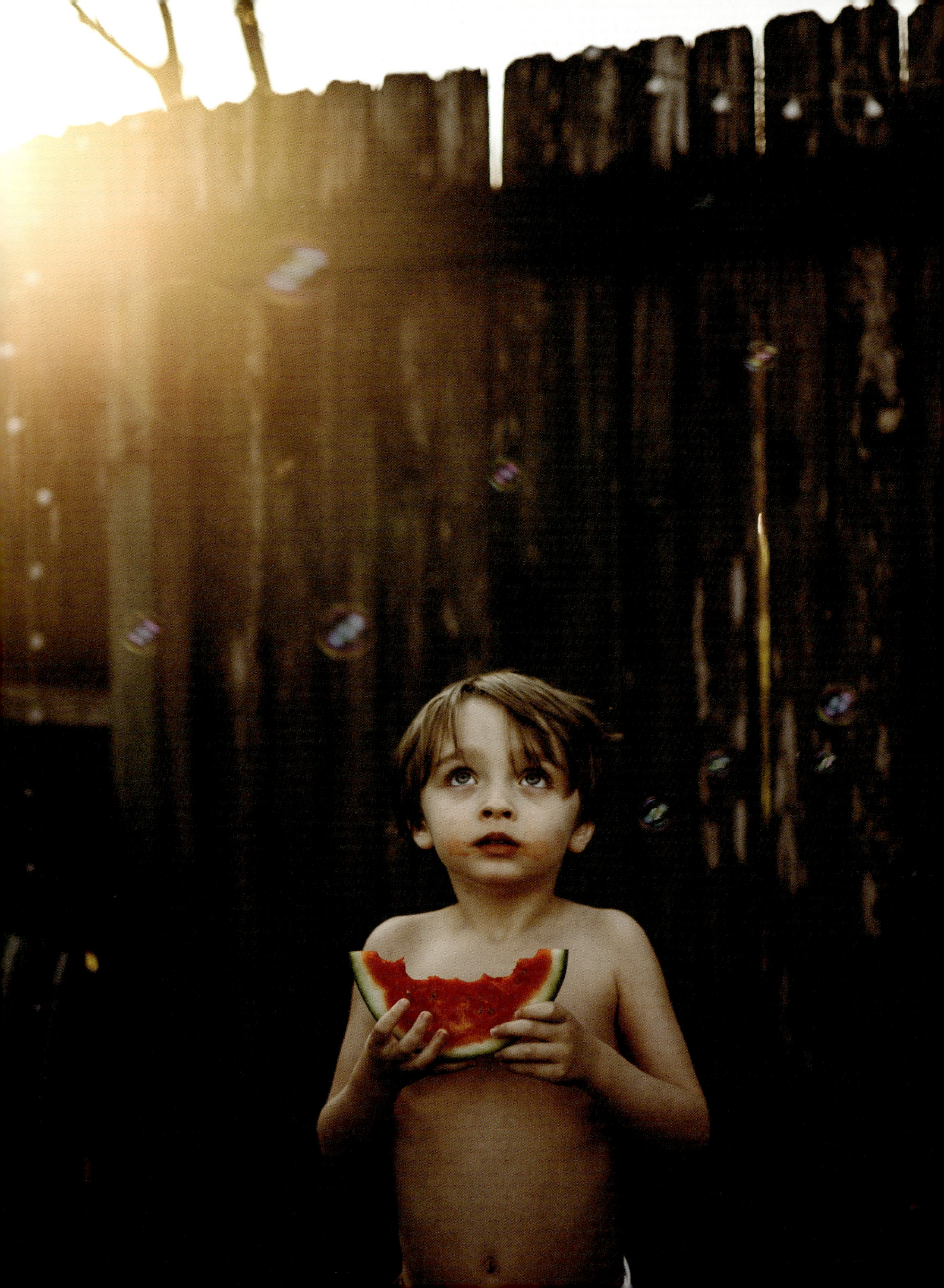

The gap is quite severe.

I do my best to focus on what Charlie can do as opposed to what he can't do. But it isn't always easy. The year following his diagnosis was a tough adjustment. Then something happened that gave me clarity, pushing me out of my dark hole and giving me the ability to support Charlie better than before. Charlie was three, and it was time to get him evaluated to see if he'd qualify for the special-needs classroom called PPCD in Texas (Preschool Program for Children with Disabilities). At that point, Charlie had been in ABA therapy for one year. His progress was slow, and his imitation skills were nonexistent, making it near impossible for him to learn new skills. He'd also scream about a hundred times per hour and had no interest in his peers whatsoever. His only interest was in putting objects in order or piling them up.

All day long, Charlie would look around the house and open every drawer and door that didn't have a lock to empty it. He'd then start to create a pile of all these things. We weren't able to leave anything out, not even our shoes. Nothing on the table, either. We added locks to all the drawers in our house just so he wouldn't empty them. We tied our chairs to the table with a string to prevent Charlie from pulling them and standing on them to get objects that were out of his reach. Meanwhile, he wasn't acknowledging us, his parents. It was as if we were completely invisible. I felt like a ghost watching him from another dimension.

As we were heading to Charlie's preschool evaluation, I already knew what the outcome was going to be.

They were going to ask those same questions they asked me at all of his evaluations, and the answers were still going to be exactly the same. No, he doesn't point. No, he doesn't answer to his name. No, he doesn't talk. No, he doesn't greet us when we come home.

As soon as we entered the building, Charlie noticed a plant and ran toward it, grabbing two hands full of dirt and dropping it on the floor, at the same time giggling uncontrollably. The speech and language pathologist (SLP) didn't look amused. We apologized profusely, and she went on to ask if this was typical behavior. We told her it was. Charlie was running everywhere in this tiny room that was not baby-proofed. He wouldn't sit down to take part in the evaluation and completely ignored all attempts from the therapist to communicate with him. The SLP skipped straight to the parent questionnaires, and she asked those

damn questions again, and even more complicated ones. Does Charlie know his colors? Can Charlie follow a one-step direction? Can Charlie follow two-step directions? In my head I'm thinking, "Really lady, if he can't follow a one-step direction, do you think he will be able to follow a two-step direction?"

At the end of the evaluation, she informed us that she wasn't able to give us any information about the testing she had just performed until she scored the questionnaires. I raised my brows, as it was obvious that Charlie was going to qualify for the special-ed classroom. We left dejected and exhausted, and I tried my best to forget about this appointment until the results came in a week later.

I had missed the phone call from the speech therapist, but she had left a voicemail. It said: "Good morning, Ms. Lamb, I rated Charlie's questionnaires and he does qualify for the PPCD program. He scored in the first percentile for receptive speech and in the second percentile for expressive speech. It's severe. The gap is quite severe. I strongly recommend that you follow through with the special-ed classroom."

I put the phone down and instantly was hit with a wave of sadness. I knew it. I didn't expect the results to be any different, but hearing from yet another professional how severe Charlie's autism was knocked me to the ground. I was heartbroken. Again. The uncertainty of his future put me into a tailspin. But when I got home and walked through the door I immediately heard Charlie laughing. When he laughs, he's just like any other kid, and it fills my heart with hope. So I wrote Charlie a letter hoping that maybe one day he will read it.

Charlie,

Today was one of those days. We got the results back from your PPCD speech assessment. They evaluated your ability to communicate. If your delays in speech and communication were significant enough, you'd be eligible to attend the special-needs classroom. I knew without a shadow of a doubt that you would qualify. Still, it hit me kinda hard when the speech therapist called back with the results. You scored in the 1st and 2nd percentiles for the two speech and communication tests. The bottom of the scale. "The gap is quite severe," she said.

You know what, Charlie? Those tests are stupid. Albert Einstein said, "If you judge a fish by its inability to climb a tree, it will live its whole life believing it is stupid."

I wish they would have evaluated your amazing ability to sort objects by size and color! I wish they'd evaluate your creativity when playing with blocks and the shapes you make. I wish they would evaluate your ability to make high towers and be so delicate when doing so. I wish they would evaluate your great taste in music.

Your inability to communicate and speak doesn't define you. Autism doesn't define you. You are unique, and you can do so much more than they saw at first glance. Let's just forget about the numbers and focus on what you can do. I have a feeling that one day you will show them—one day you will tell them what you can really do.

I hope he never forgives you.

Throughout the years, I've been putting in a bigger effort in trying to see the glass half-full with Charlie. Raising a child with nonverbal autism is a balancing act. Too much hope, and you take the risk of being disappointed. Not enough, and you prevent happiness from entering your life.

Recently, I shared on Facebook an update on Charlie's language development. Charlie had repeated the word "daddy" several times, leaving us speechless. We had been waiting for Charlie to say something for five years, so I was really excited to share the news with my followers. But wouldn't you know that as soon as I expressed a bit of hope, the #ActuallyAutistic gang showed up again. This time they were critical of my use of the word "thief" to describe autism. In my post, I had shared that I was over the moon about Charlie's breakthrough but that a part of me was scared that autism was going to take this skill away from Charlie one more time. Charlie's first regression was crushing, and I didn't want to go through the same heartbreak. It turned out that I was

right to be afraid. This breakthrough, while amazing, didn't last. Charlie plateaued and eventually regressed again.

Some of the comments from the #ActuallyAutistic on my post made me rather angry. I'm not the perfect mom. I have hard days, but I love Charlie, and I always will. According to them, I'm a martyr mom. They believe parents aren't allowed to express any morsel of negativity unless their child dies. "Laugh away Eileen Lamb, you should be ashamed, seeking pity for being ashamed of your nonverbal son. I hope he never forgives you." Someone else wrote, "You are not welcome in the autism community, your son will be when he grows up. We are all talking about you and will never forget your name." I suppose it was wrong of me to think they would leave me alone once I made my autism diagnosis public.

I paused to take their critique seriously. I asked myself, how would I feel if my mom had shared my autism journey with the world without asking? What if she had shared in a blog about

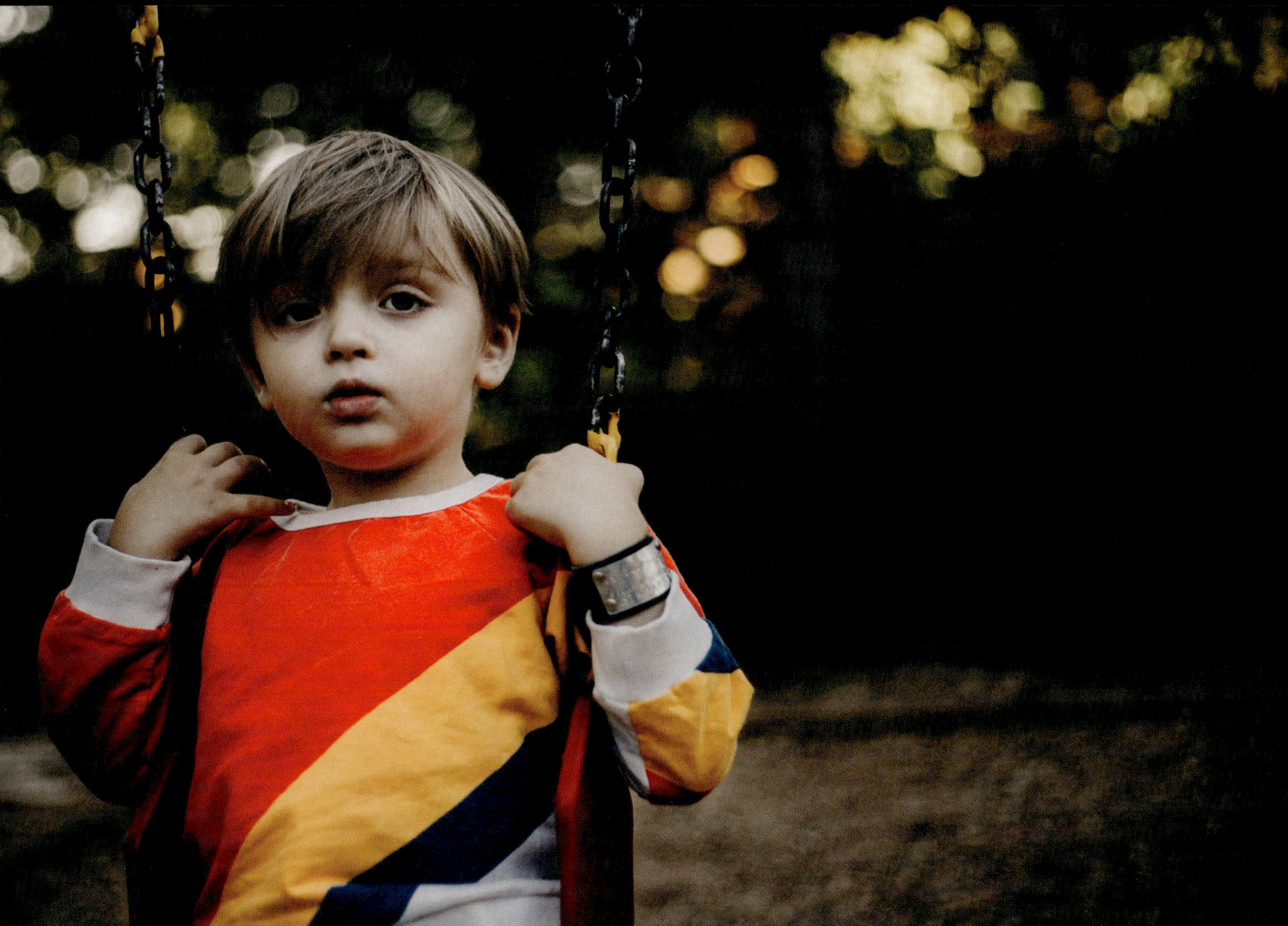

what raising a child with high-functioning autism was like for her from her perspective? As long as she still loved me as she does, I think I would be so proud of her for opening up and showing the world that autism is nothing to be ashamed of. We need to hear from people with autism, but we also need more voices of people affected by autism, who raise, live with, are friends with, and are even married to people on the spectrum. I would have been touched that she cared enough about me to talk about a subject so taboo in France.

We live in an age where people online expect nothing short of perfection and are quick to judge. It's all black or white. There's no appreciation for balance, nuance; there's no in between.

I wish people understood that you can be sad about your child being severely disabled and still love him with every fiber of your being.

But the critics aren't going to stop me from sharing Charlie's or my autism journey. The overwhelming support I receive, the people I've helped with my blog, they make it all worthwhile.

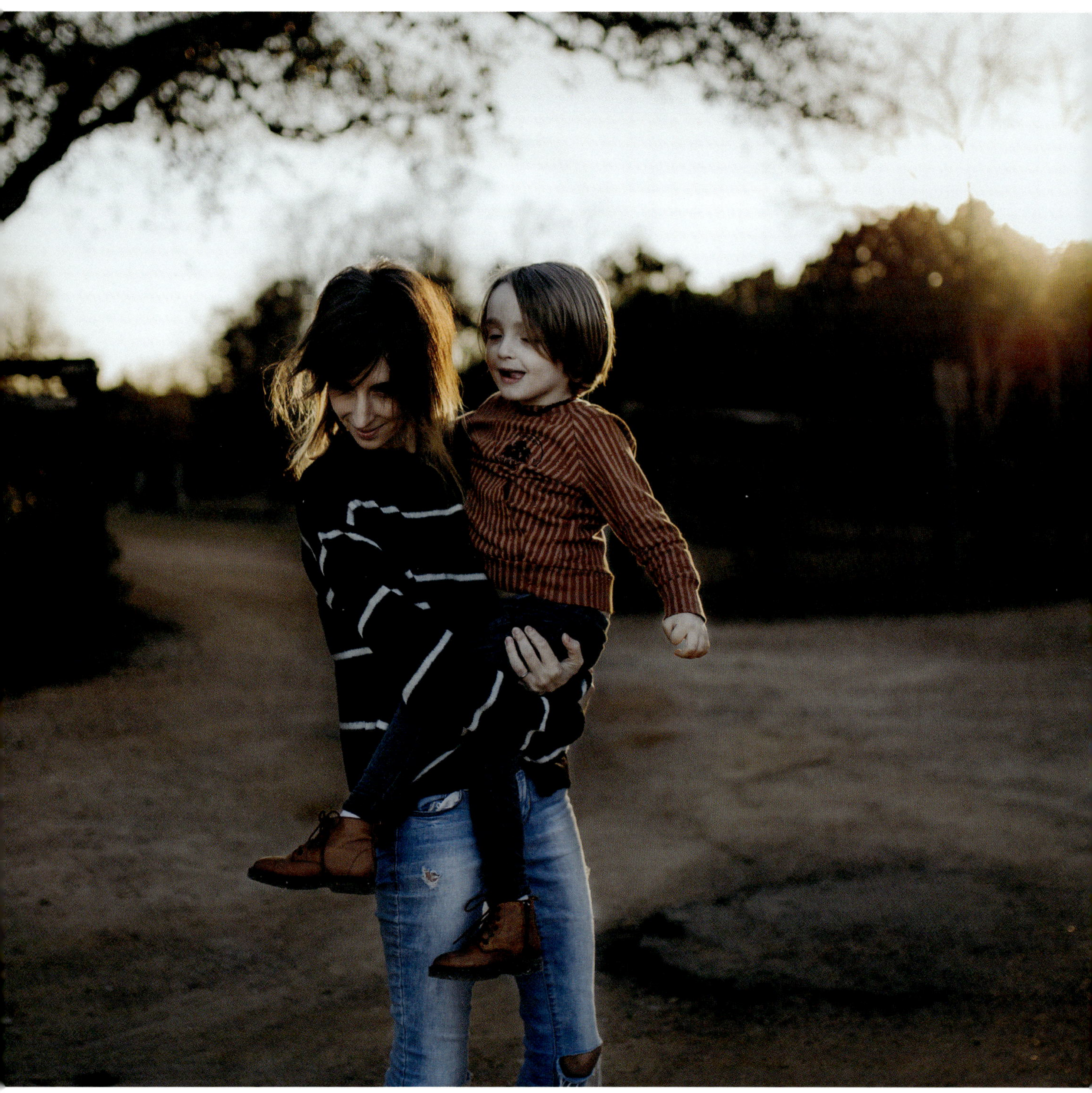

Are you sure I'm autistic?

We all strive to be accepted. It's a pretty universal desire, a fundamental and often even central need in people's lives. Wanting to be part of a group is in our nature. It helps us feel safe and protected. I've always felt a strong need to belong but have experienced rejection more than camaraderie in my time. And it doesn't get any easier.

After my diagnosis, I thought I was going to finally have a tribe. I thought I would naturally fit in with other autistic adults, people who struggle with the same fundamental things as me, who understand what it's like to have an invisible disability. Although I knew that there was a vocal group of autistic adults who didn't share my views on autism, I didn't realize how difficult it would be to meet autistic adults who would accept me. I soon began to understand that they weren't the minority. I was.

Autism explained everything I've always struggled with, but instead of feeling relieved to have answers about myself, I felt more alienated than ever before. If I didn't belong with autistic adults like me, then where was my place? I wondered if Dr. Robble was wrong. I had heard about people being misdiagnosed… what if that happened to me, too? As the doubt started to consume me, I asked Dr. Robble: "Are you sure I'm autistic?"

Back when I scheduled my therapeutic assessment, I made sure to choose an expert in autism. I wanted to meet with a professional who wouldn't make a mistake, a doctor trusted in the autism field who would spend a lot of time with me before coming to a decision. Dr. Robble is respected as a specialist in the field, so I was thrilled to find her. When I confessed my doubts to her, she reminded me that she doesn't issue autism diagnoses easily. She was certain I was autistic, and she assured me I was not misdiagnosed. I felt disappointed.

Perhaps when I asked Dr. Robble for confirmation that I was autistic, I was really hoping she'd change her mind and diagnose me with a condition whose surrounding community would be nicer and more welcoming. I thought seeking a diagnosis would be a way for me to find my tribe, but it didn't work. I'm still lonely in that regard. I find comfort in writing, and I share my story with the hope that someone might reach out to me and relate—someone who's autistic but not too angry at the rest of the world. I often feel like I'm too autistic for neurotypical people and not irritated enough with the rest of the population to fit in with autistic adults. I want to find my place.

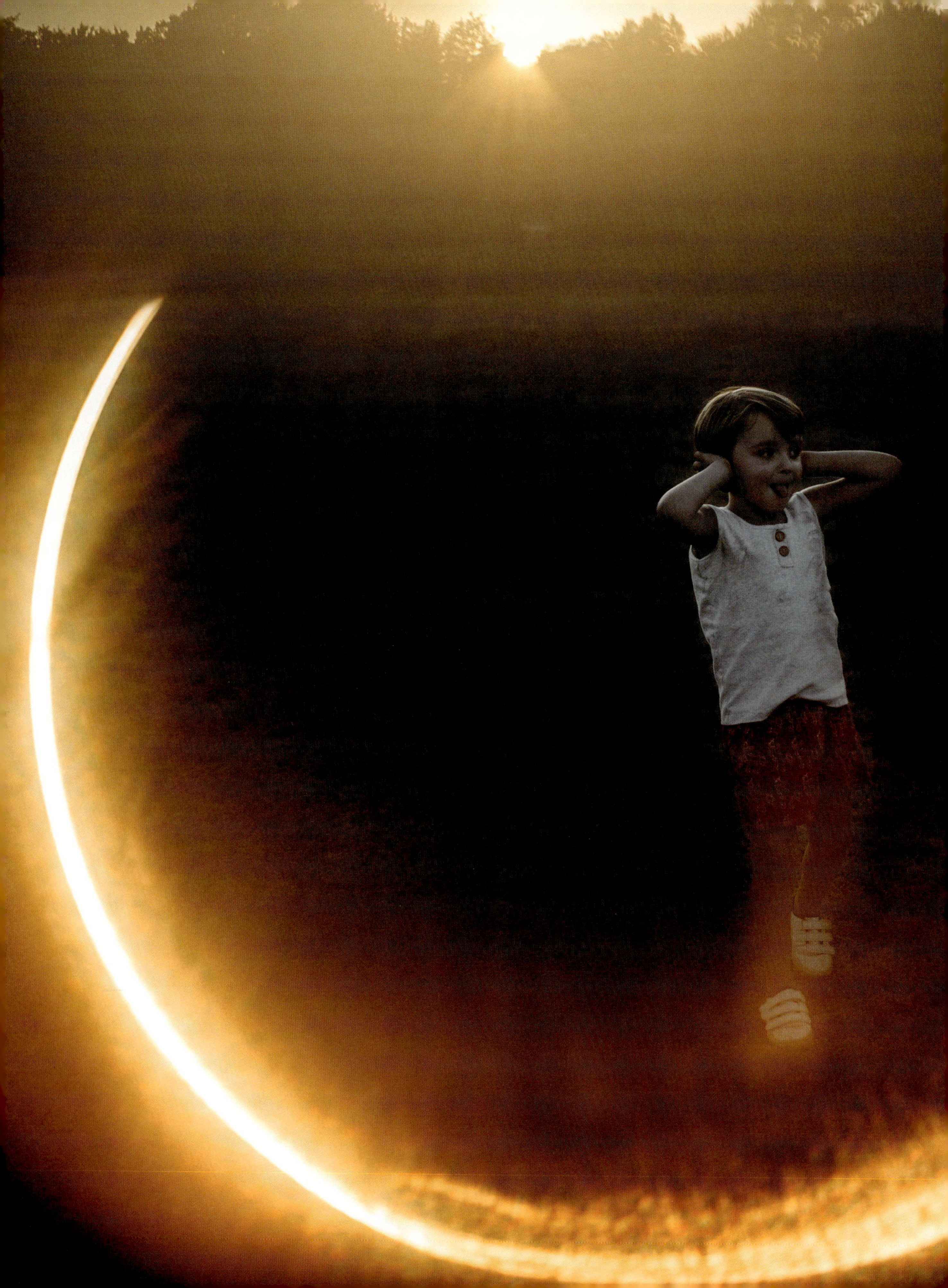

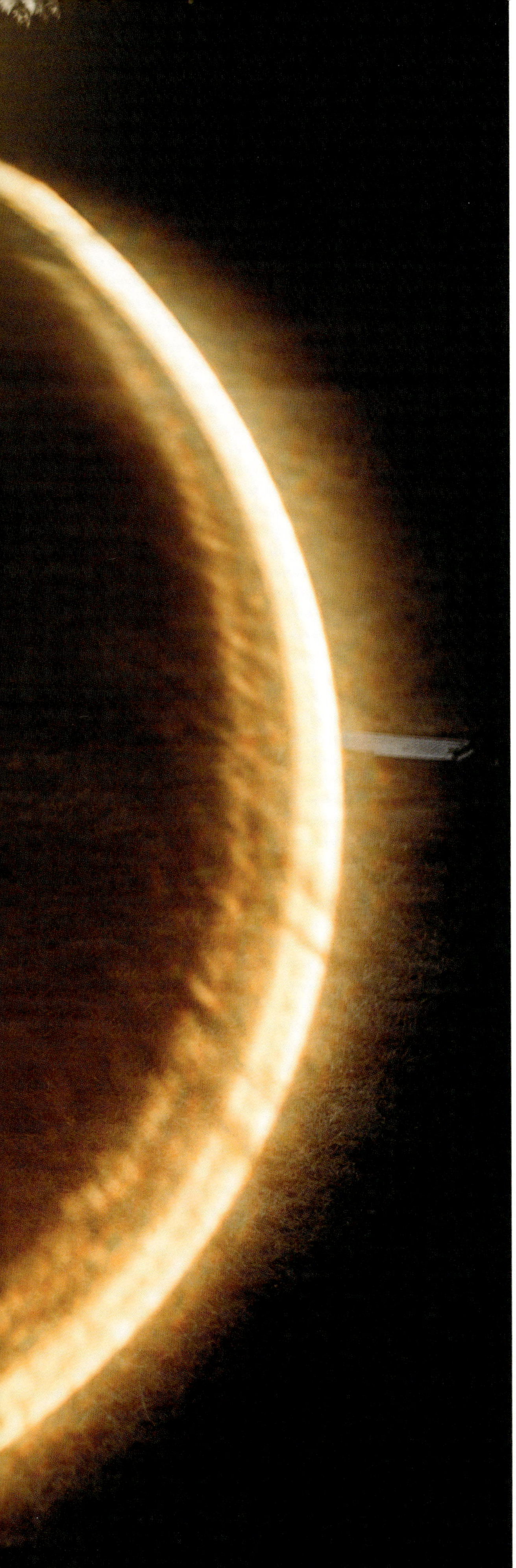

> # It's okay
> # to grieve.

When my therapist said those words, "It's okay to grieve," I felt like a weight had been lifted off my shoulders. The guilt that had been torturing me for years started to fade away. My feelings were normal, after all. Dr. Robble explained that all the parents of severely autistic children she sees have similar feelings. They feel powerless, defeated, frustrated, and depressed. I've felt all these emotions. I'd kept them to myself for a while because I was ashamed of feeling this way. I was afraid to admit these feelings, even to my husband. I love my little boy, my Charlie, so the sadness that engulfed me in that moment was confusing. For a long time, I buried it. I never mentioned it, particularly on my blog knowing that there, I'd be open to criticism. People on the internet were already critiquing me, so sharing that I was grieving the child I thought I was going to have would have been like offering myself up on a silver platter.

The truth is that raising a nonverbal autistic child is emotionally draining. I wish I could say that I was strong enough that Charlie's severe impairments didn't affect me, but I'm not. It breaks my heart to see Charlie struggling daily. It's hard for Charlie, who can't communicate beyond basic needs such as "I want water," but it's also hard on us, his parents. When Charlie was diagnosed, many dreams went out the window.

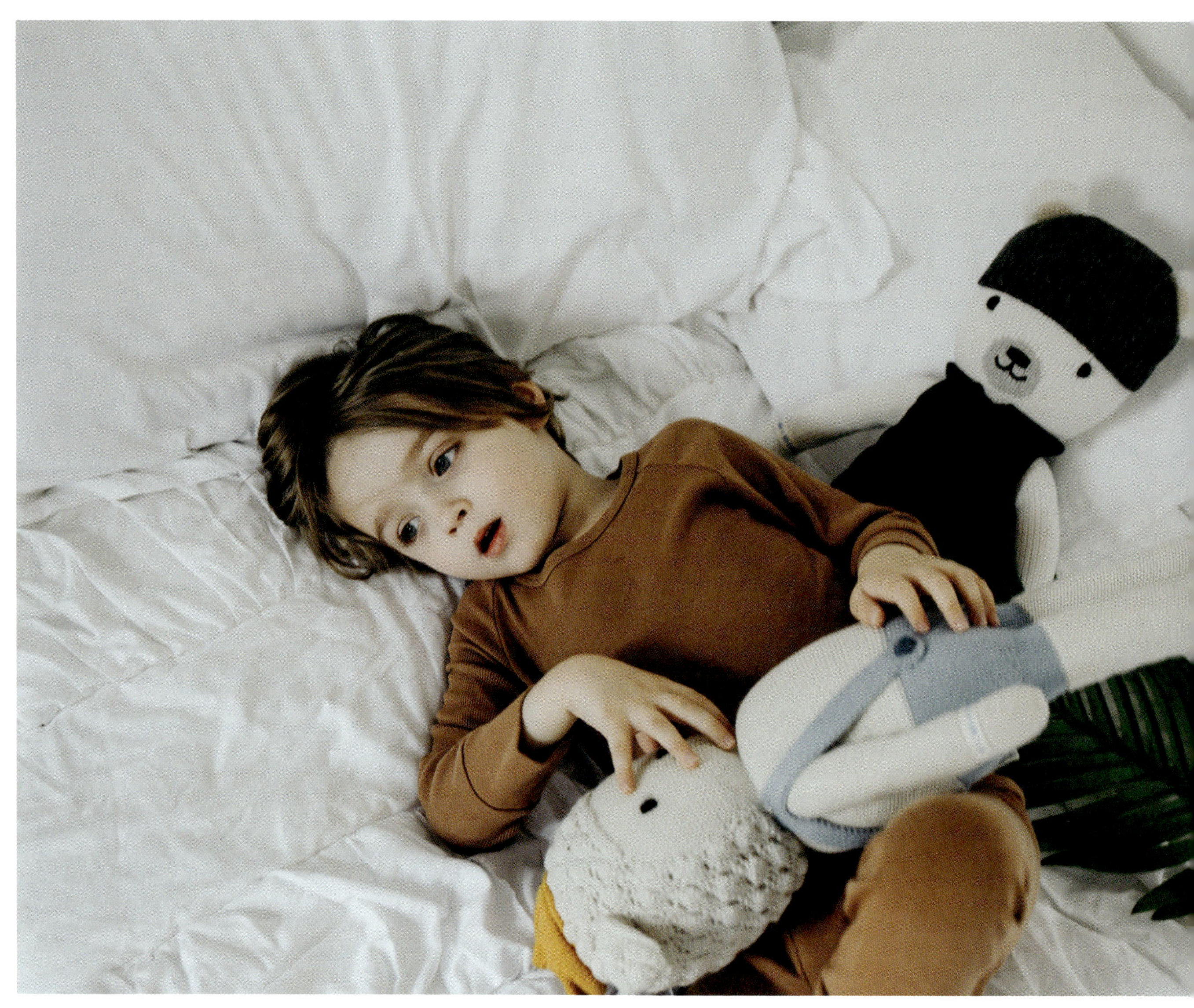

All of my expectations and everything I'd imagined doing with my child were gone.

I once dreamed about having philosophical discussions with Charlie and long talks about soccer and outer space and just life in general. I now simply long to hear him call me "mommy" or say "I love you" purposely, even just once.

Besides very basic needs, which he conveys using an app on his iPad, Charlie is unable to make himself understood. It's like that recurring nightmare where you're in danger and you're screaming with all your might, but no sound comes out. I used to have that nightmare all the time as a child. That feeling of powerlessness is paralyzing. I wonder if sometimes Charlie feels powerless? As his mom, it's my job to protect him and I want to make things easier for him, I want to help. I want to fix his inability to communicate. I don't want to fix him. I want to fix his broken voice. I wish someone would invent some kind of brain decoder, something that would allow me to understand him and make it all better because that's what moms do. We make it better. But I can't. Grieving something means realizing you can't change it. I'm grieving my inability to encourage my child's development like other mothers are able to do.

When Charlie needs something and I'm unable to understand what it is, it's the most powerless feeling. I usually spend a few minutes showing him various objects and food items around the house in hopes that he'll want one of them. When I'm wrong—and that happens often—he gets frustrated.

Cereal? Pushes it away.
Juice? Pushes it away.
Toast? Pushes it away.
Yogurt? Pushes it away.

You can feel the intensity of our growing frustration as I fail to comprehend what he wants to eat. He gets infinitely more impatient with each wrong guess. The restlessness, the grunts, and then the quiet whines. Believe me, Charlie. I'm trying as hard as I can to get you what you want, but I can't because I don't know what it is. Eventually, we've exhausted all our options, and this is usually the moment when tears slowly start rolling down his face and he resorts to screaming. I feel sad and frustrated, too. And once again powerless. Once we've reached that point, there's nothing else I can do. I've failed, and now we just have to wait. I wait until I hear the silence. Not the kind of silence you want to hear. It's a silence full of tension. A silence that means that Charlie has given up because that's the only thing he can do. No matter how hard he tries, he can't communicate and he can't make himself heard. The only thing he can do now is surrender.

Still, I love Charlie. All of him. The way he is. I simultaneously don't want to change him and do. I'm not grieving him. I'm grieving my dreams of him. I'm grieving the dreams I had of Charlie as a seven-year-old, sitting next to me outside at sunset, debating which Pokémon is a better starter option in Pokémon Blue. I'm grieving my youth, the naiveté that led me to believe that all moms get to hear their child call them mommy in a purposeful way, the innocence that tricked me into believing that all children love and cling to their parents. I'm grieving the dream of speaking French with Charlie and secretly laughing at the first putain he pronounces. I'm not grieving you, Charlie. I'm grieving my dreams.

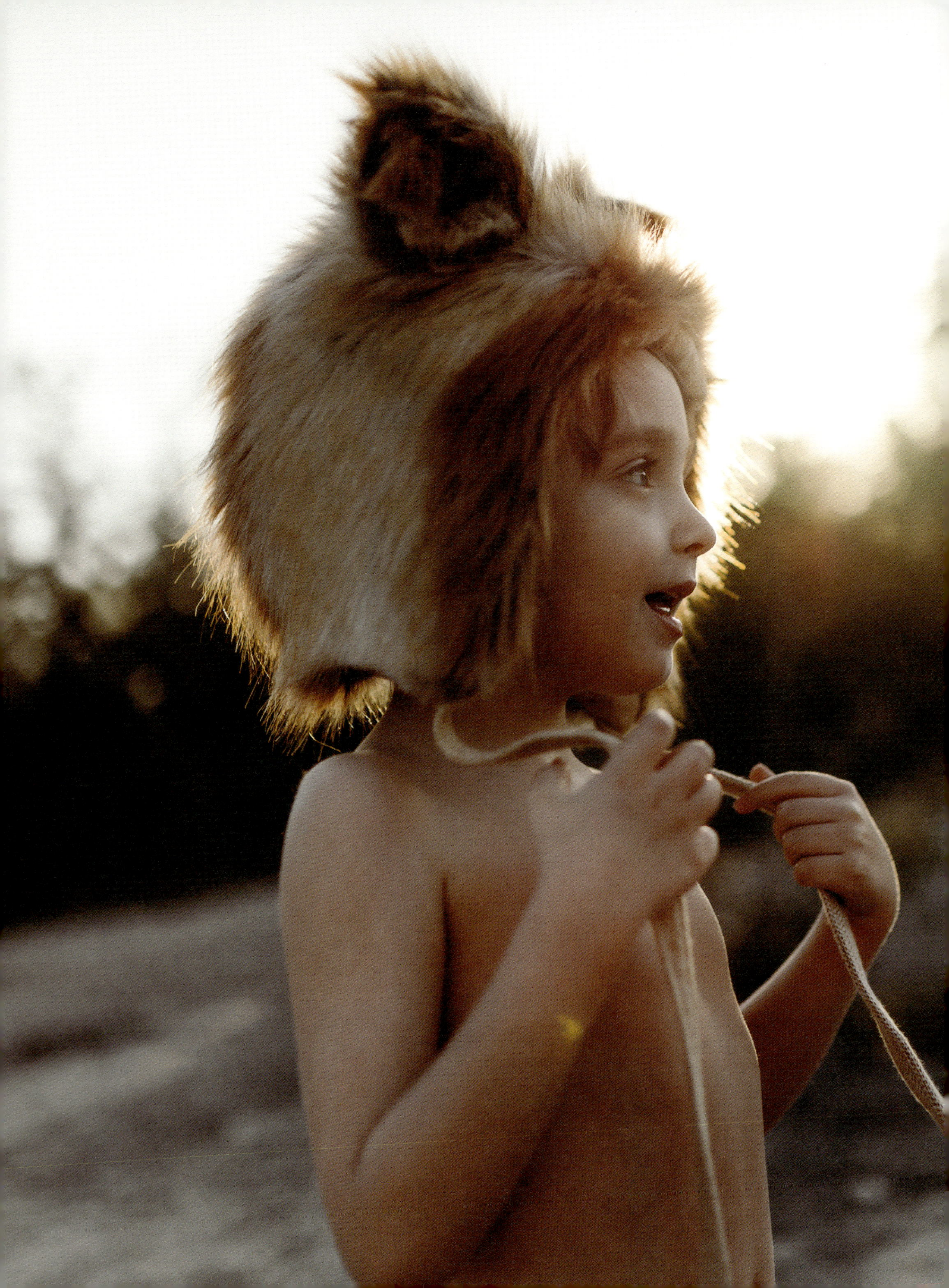

" Mommy! **"**

With autism, I always feel like I'm playing a balancing act, trying to find a happy medium with everything. The balance between espousing autism acceptance and also making sure that people realize that autism is a disability. There are beautiful moments of sincere hope and more sobering moments reminding you to be realistic with your expectations. I remember some initial feelings of pure happiness and hope after Charlie spoke for the first time. I wanted to believe we had turned a corner. This was finally it: Charlie was going to start communicating and the past five years would just become a distant memory of an old lifetime. A struggle that was no longer mine. I imagined myself looking back on tougher times with a smile, knowing they had been put to bed. I could almost see it. Almost feel it.

But I also remember the nagging doubt, the feeling that this was too good to be true and that his breakthrough could just be another blip on the radar, not to resurface for a long time to come. That's what autism does. It gives you what you want for a few days, weeks, maybe months, and then it takes it away. Cruel. Heartless. It gives just so it can take.

I try not to hang my happiness on those moments of progress anymore. I feel it, try to let it warm every fiber of my body for a day; two if I'm lucky, and then let go. I let it go. Experience has taught me that progress with Charlie has an expiration date, like a hot summer-camp romance. It's the best thing in the entire world in that moment and you relish every fleeting second because you know it will come to an end and you'll be left heartbroken.

The first time Charlie said "mommy," it was just incredible. I couldn't believe my ears. Did this beautiful child of mine standing in front of me finally realize how deep my love for him was? Did he realize that I exist and feel the deep connection we share that I'd been feeling since months before he was even born? No, I don't think he did. After the euphoria of the first few "mommys" faded away, it dawned on me: Charlie doesn't know I'm his mommy. He doesn't know that is my name. He repeats the word because that's what he's learned to do, but the meaning beyond the word, the emotion, the connection, just isn't there. There's no running to mommy if he stubs his toe nor asking for a hug because he needs comfort. There's no saying "mommy" unless someone asks him to repeat it, and there are never any tears when I leave him. Ever. I know that I'm his mommy, and I wonder if he knows it, too.

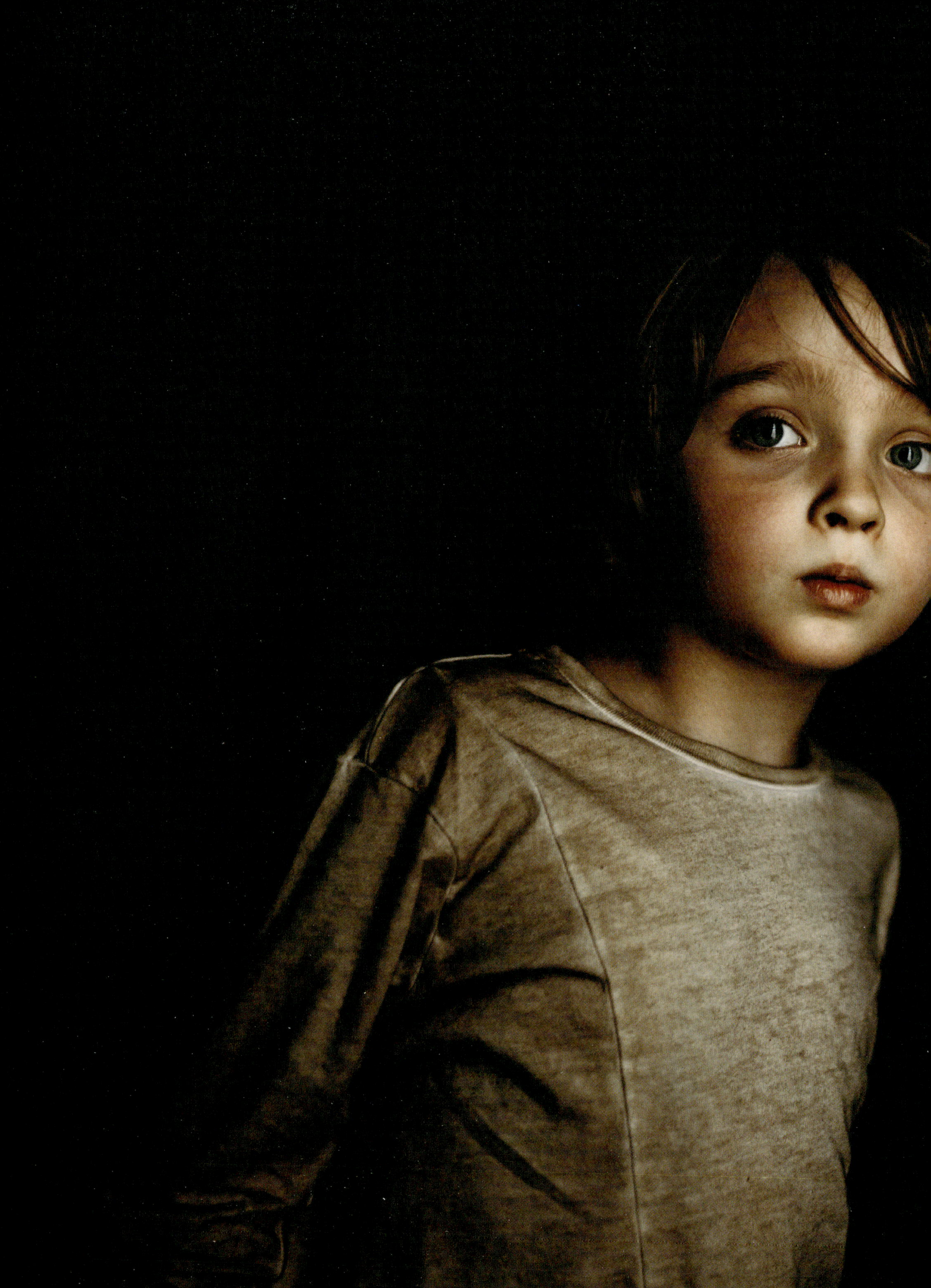

Maybe it's selfish. Maybe I shouldn't care so much about Charlie calling me mommy. But I do. "Mommy." It's so much more than just a word. It's an earned title, a reward. It's the validation that the little human you created cares about you enough to give you a name, and even more, enough to use it. A name that's yours forever. I crumbled to pieces when I realized that Charlie was just mindlessly repeating the word. I felt sad. I still do. But as the mother of a severely autistic child, I'm expected to stay strong or expose myself to the less-than-glorious title of "martyr mom."

These expectations can be hard on us parents of autistic children. That pressure to be the perfect mom, the perfect dad, at all times, it's heavy and I often feel myself crumbling under the weight of it all. Many of us lack the resources and support to help our children and deal with our feelings. We need support and understanding, too. We do our best, and when we don't succeed, we're the first to be disappointed in ourselves. We don't need a reminder from strangers that we failed. I feel love, I feel pride, but sometimes I feel despair, heartbreak, and shame. And that's okay.

Charlie is Charlie. I really do believe in my heart that Charlie knows that I love him no matter what. Verbal, nonverbal, autistic, neurotypical…I don't care. If he never calls me mommy intentionally, I will still love him just as much. My imperfections, needs, and wants don't make me a bad mom—they make me human.

How can you be autistic and still use functioning labels?

As I kept sharing about autism on my blog, the #ActuallyAutistic doubled down on their attacks. They were now angry at me for describing myself as being high-functioning autistic as opposed to just autistic.

Functioning labels are used to give more information about the functioning level of people on the autism spectrum. The terms are broad and they take into consideration things like verbal and self-care abilities. However, some people believe that functioning labels can be hurtful. The main criticism is that when you create this division, the deficits of people considered high-functioning are ignored, and so are the abilities of people considered low-functioning.

The thing is, though, there is a big difference between people on each end of the spectrum. Making no distinction between Charlie's and my autism will just create confusion. I use functioning labels because I want people to understand how broad the spectrum is and how different each autistic individual's abilities and struggles are.

Charlie is level 3 autistic, which is the most severe. Level 1 autistic people like me can be gently guided into appropriate social behavior and communication. Charlie doesn't even know there's something to learn, so at this point in time, he can't learn. For instance, I can communicate. I'm able to form relationships. I don't naturally know how to act in social situations, but I've learned how. It's tiring, but I can do it. I don't like big social gatherings and crowds, I don't tolerate noise very well. But if I have help, I can rise to the occasion. To "pass." High-functioning autistic people can learn. And even though sometimes despite my best effort, I can't pass, I remind myself that people on the other end of the spectrum, like Charlie, would most likely never pass as typical, no matter how hard they try.

I do understand why in some cases, functioning labels may be confusing. They give the general public the impression that one autistic person will function on that same level every day and in every situation. In reality, an autistic person may be able to pass as neurotypical in certain situations and have a complete melt-down in another. Or they may be able to earn a high salary using a "splinter skill" but also may not be able to tie their shoes. We are all different from each other, and our ability to pass may change based on time, environment, and mood.

It can be said that people on the low end of the spectrum have more difficulties, fewer abilities, and greater struggles. But perhaps the self-awareness of higher functioning people can lead to them having greater subjective difficulty with their struggles, even though from the outside it might seem like those struggles are much less severe. Additionally, people on

That said, as an adult-diagnosed autistic raising a nonverbal child, I see both sides of the spectrum every day and find functioning labels important.

Even on my worst day, I will never struggle as much as Charlie on a good day.

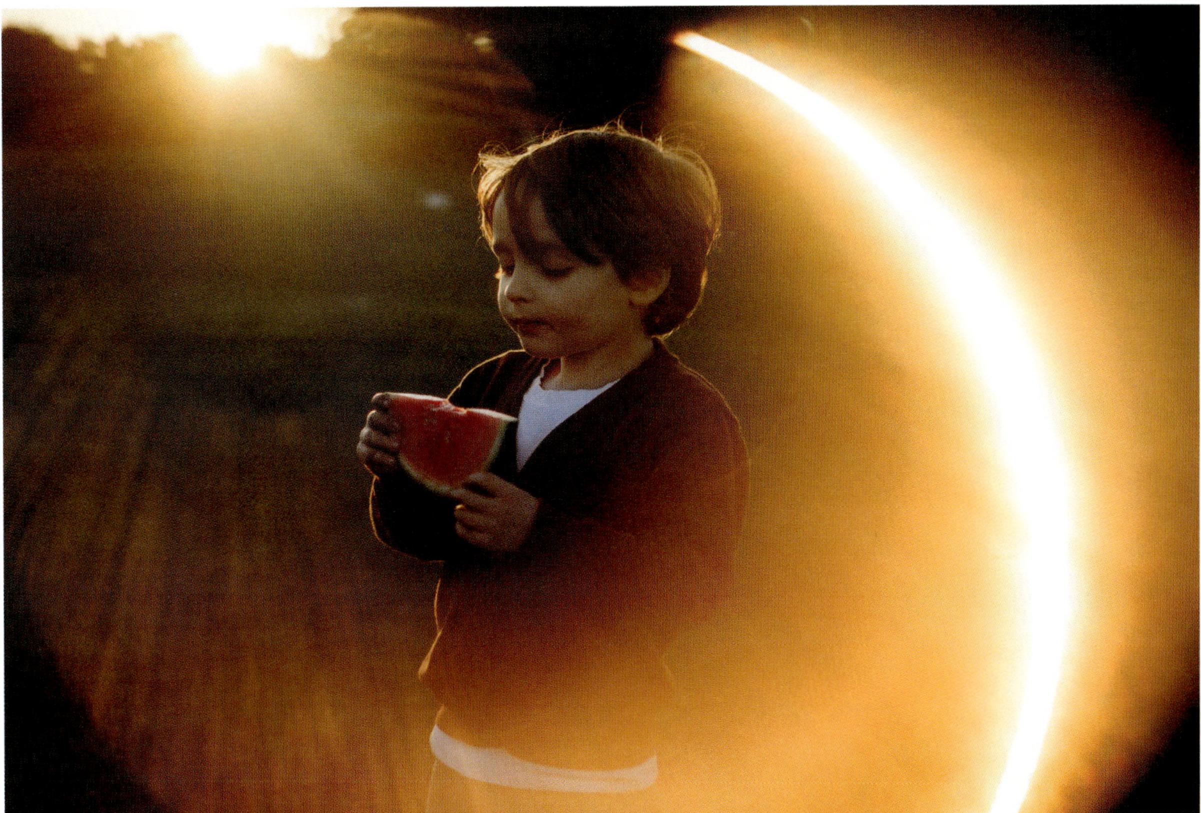

the high-functioning side of the spectrum can feel misunderstood because their disabilities aren't as obvious as someone who's on the severe side of the spectrum.

Functioning labels help people better understand how two people with very different abilities and struggles can both be autistic.

Lift the Handle

Going to the store isn't the only errand I wish I could run without feeling drained. I can count on one hand the number of times I've been able to get gas without encountering an issue. A few months ago, I was on my way to drop Charlie off at therapy when I saw the warning that had probably been staring at me for a while already: "0 miles range remaining." I usually would have risked running out of gas just so I could fill up at the one gas station I'm familiar with, but not this time. I gave myself a pep talk and stopped by a random gas station on my way.

I kicked off stepping out of my comfort zone by pulling up to the pump on the wrong side. Not a big deal. I'm sure that happens to everyone. I kept my enthusiasm up while doing that embarrassing backing out and turning around maneuver, finally backing into the spot the correct way. Except not! I stepped out of the car and somehow the pump was still on the wrong side. Oh my god, I thought. How did that happen?

Finally, I fixed it, but it was now time to pay at the pump and damn it! The screen was totally different than the one at the other gas station. I tried swiping my card, but no luck. Inserting it? No luck, either. I hold it in front of the screen—maybe it's some kind of new technology? But no, no luck there, either. The screen keeps showing an error message. Alright, still no big deal, I'm okay. I head inside the gas station to pay.

I'm now back outside ready to fill up, but as I put the nozzle into the tank and squeeze the handle, no gas comes out. I press the button again and even try to get a different kind of gas, but still, nothing happens. The pump is also different from the one near my house. There is a sign that says "lift the handle," but I can't see any handles. Channeling all the adaptability skills I learned in the past, I attempt to lift everything that can possibly be a handle. Nothing is moving. I'm now thoroughly embarrassed. I don't want to go back inside a second time to ask for help, but after a minute of inspecting the pump, not being able to get gas, I resign myself to do it. I ask the guy behind the counter for help. "Hi, I can't figure out how to pump the gas." The man barely looks at me and says, "Lift the handle." Thanks, man, that's super helpful, I thought. That's exactly what the sign says. I ask him to specify, "Which handle?" He then vaguely points in the direction of the pump without saying a word. That's not exactly helpful, either, but I take the hint that he doesn't want to help me. I go back outside and again lift everything I can. Nothing moves, so I Google it on the spot. Nope, not helpful, either.

At this point, I have been at the gas station for 10 minutes, and the cars waiting in line behind me are now maneuvering to find a different pump. I'm feeling frustrated with the guy inside and disappointed in myself for not being able to figure this out. I go back inside for the third time telling the guy behind the counter that his pump must be broken because I still haven't been able to get gas. He doesn't say anything to me and asks the guy waiting to pay for his candy bar to "please go help the lady." So, I head back to the pump with a complete stranger who casually lifts a handle at the base of where the nozzle is rested, puts the nozzle in the tank for me, and finally, the gas starts flowing. Mind blown.

I'm able to laugh it off now, but it's always frustrating when I step out of my comfort zone and fail. That felt like failing a big exam. But I was proud of myself for trying, and just like with every other failure I went through, I learned something. I know now what they mean by "lift the handle." Yeah, you have to lift the handle.

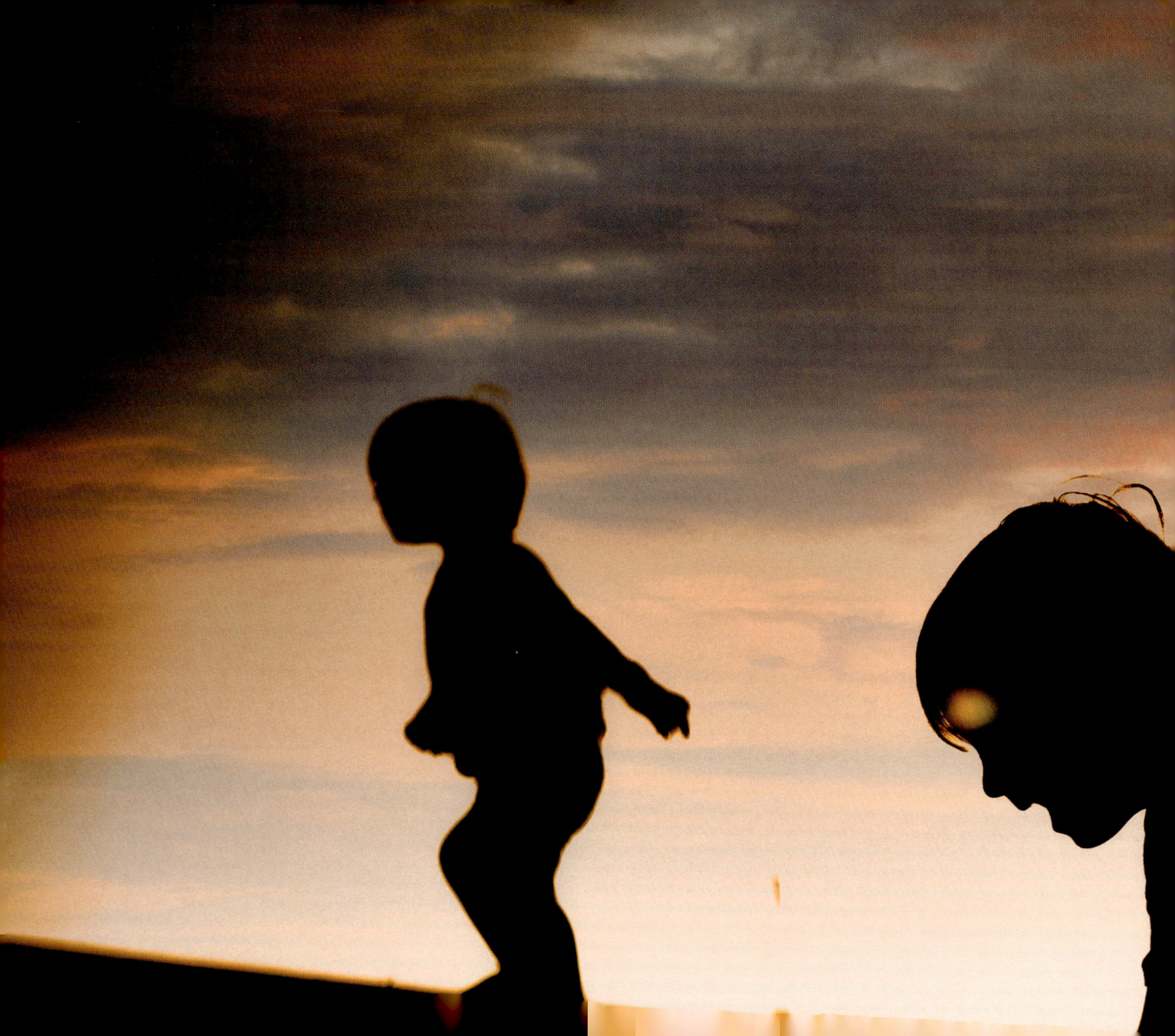

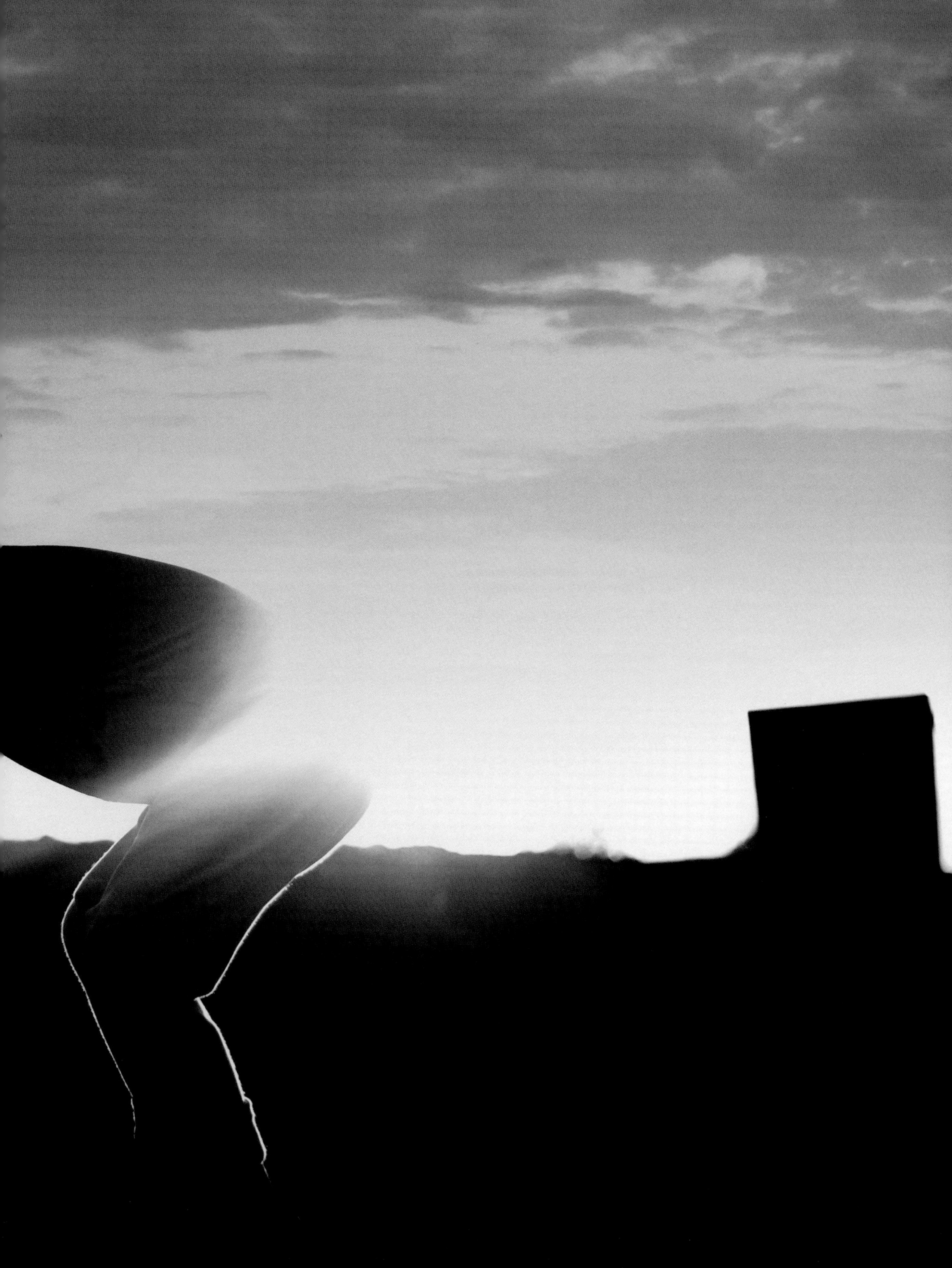

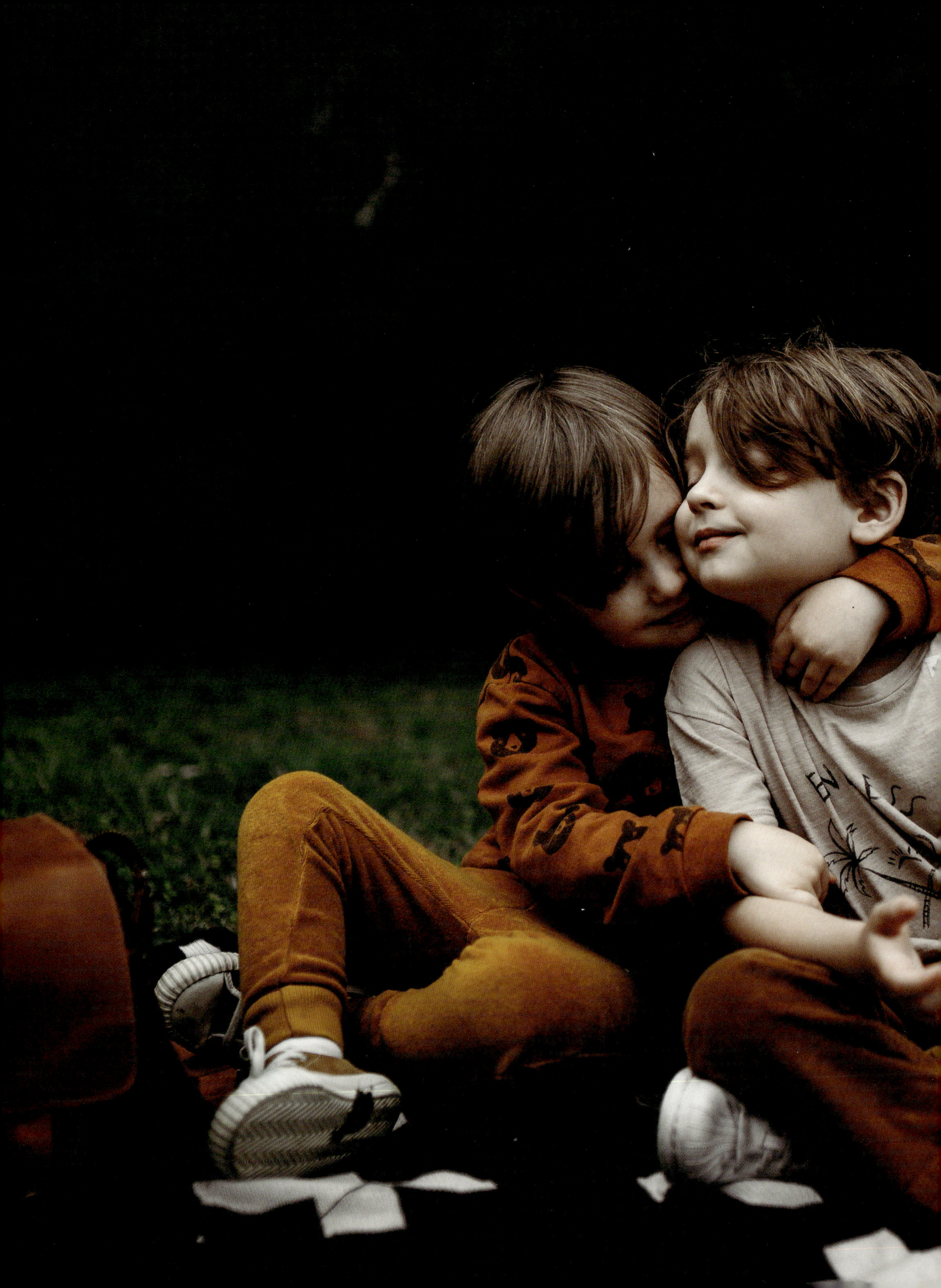

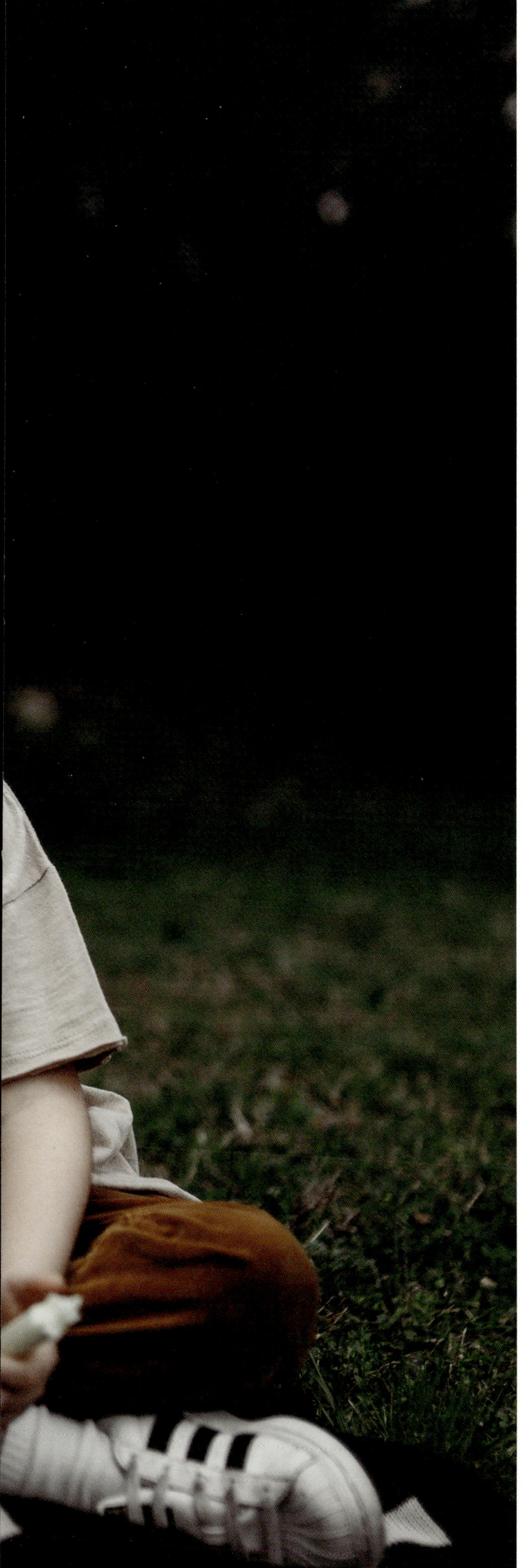

Brothers

Growing up, I always wanted a big brother. I wanted a best friend. A friend who wouldn't be able to leave me if I accidentally hurt their feelings. Someone I could argue with, someone who would have my back when I got bullied, someone to stand up for me. I know siblings' relationship can be a touchy one, too, but I've always been envious of my friends who had big brothers. I was eight years old when I came to peace with the fact that it probably wasn't possible for my parents to give birth to a big brother for me, so I amended my request to a little brother. That never happened, either. I'm an only child.

When I found out I was pregnant with Jude, my youngest, I was excited. I was going to give the boys what I'd dreamt of as a child. They'd both have a brother they could count on. During my pregnancy, just like with Charlie, I spent a lot of time fantasizing about what the future would be like with my two boys. I kept thinking about the moment when Charlie would meet Jude. I thought he'd fall in love with his brother instantly, giving him a sweet little kiss on the forehead as soon as he saw him at the hospital. I imagined Charlie protecting Jude and teaching him how to build big towers. I pictured him watching over Jude because that's what big brothers do. There was no doubt in my mind that Charlie was going to be the perennial winner of the "Best Big Brother" award.

And then it happened: Charlie was diagnosed with autism a few months into my pregnancy with Jude.

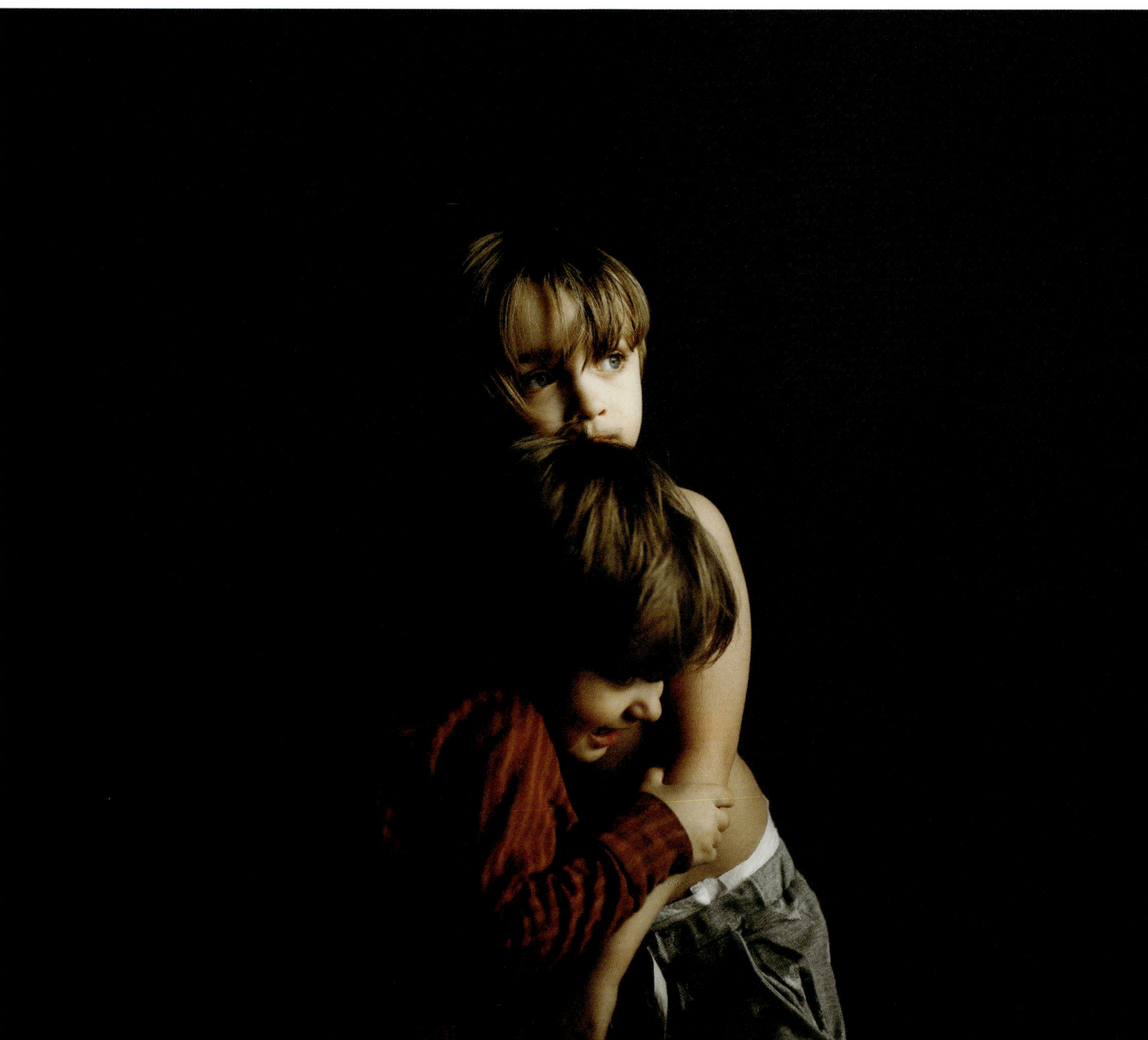

Week after week, he regressed. He lived in a world of his own and we couldn't access him anymore—there were no more words, rare smiles, and lots of tantrums, meltdowns, and piercing screams. Was Charlie ready to be a big brother?

My due date wasn't until the end of July, but we had joked that Jude was going to be born on Independence Day to please his America-loving mom, and he was. Jude was born on July 4th, three weeks early and healthy as can be. He had a head full of dark hair and big blue eyes. We were off to a great start, I thought.

At the hospital, I was excited for Charlie to meet Jude, but he didn't even look at his little brother. It was as if Jude was completely invisible. Charlie's eyes weren't even looking in his direction. Eventually, after a few days at home, Charlie noticed him. Jude's cries were hard to ignore. Charlie would scream and cover his ears in response to Jude making any sort of noise at all. A few times, Charlie even slapped his brother in the face. My heart was broken.

Over time, the screams lessened, but Charlie still refused to interact with Jude. Ignorance was better than aggression. A step in the right direction, we thought. But sometimes, I worry that Charlie's attitude towards Jude is affecting him. I'm sensitive to being rejected, so I wonder if it's hard for Jude, too, feeling like Charlie doesn't want to be around him. I remember capturing this bittersweet photo of them and sharing it on social media with this caption:

At first glance, it's just two children fighting. If you look closely, though, you'll notice Jude's pouty face. He's sad. He wanted Charlie to play with him. How do you explain autism to a two-year-old? Jude is a social butterfly. He likes to talk and be with people. He doesn't understand yet that his brother has different needs and always will. Charlie is covering his ears protecting himself from Jude's incessant requests to play, but Jude doesn't understand that so he keeps begging:

"Charlie! Pleassse play! Charlie!"

That's the cycle we get into. Jude wants to play, Charlie doesn't, so Jude screams, which upsets Charlie even more and makes Jude just overall confused about the situation.

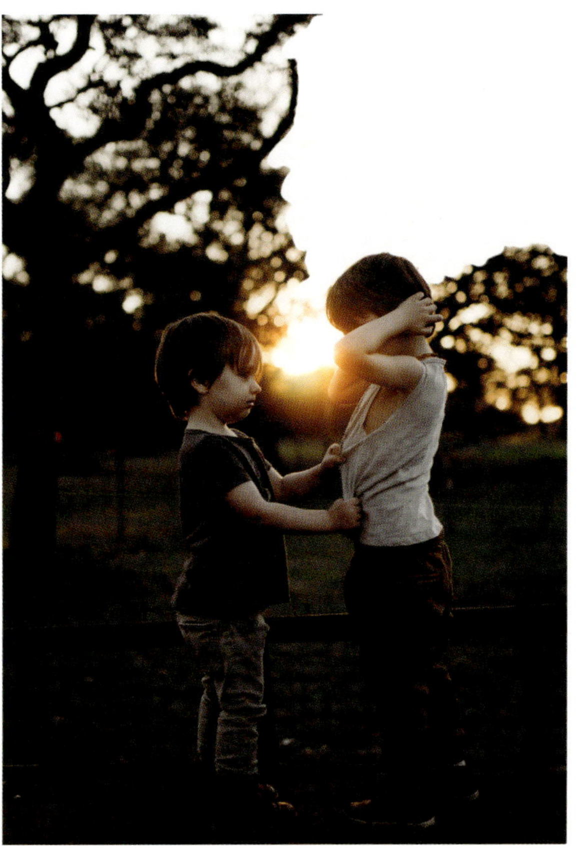

All brothers fight. But still, it's bittersweet because I wonder if they'll ever be able to enjoy a conversation together. I wonder if Jude will ever get an answer from Charlie.

Since I posted this photo, Jude's understanding of Charlie's needs has blossomed. While it breaks my heart to see Jude sad when Charlie rejects him, I also see all the amazing ways in which having Charlie as a big brother has a positive impact on him. He seems to accept differences in people in the most natural way. He's compassionate and always wants people around him to be happy. He's the kind of child who comes to you and asks if you're okay if you look sad. I have the feeling Jude will be a loyal friend, the kind of friend I'd want to have who'd stick it out during the good and bad—a patient, loving, and understanding friend. I also love the way Jude understands that certain situations are overwhelming for Charlie even if they're not overwhelming to him, like when things get too loud and he covers Charlie's ears with his chubby little cupped hands to block out the noise. His big heart awes me, and when I witness these moments, I know that everything will be okay. Because they have each other.

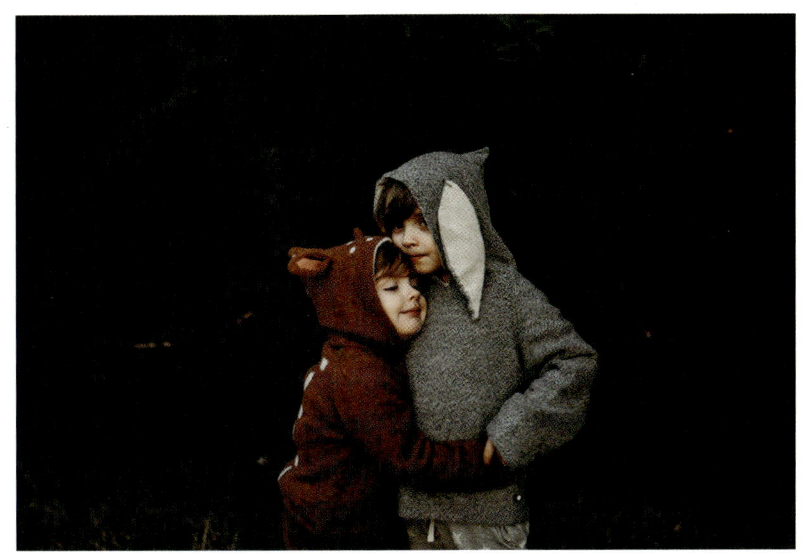

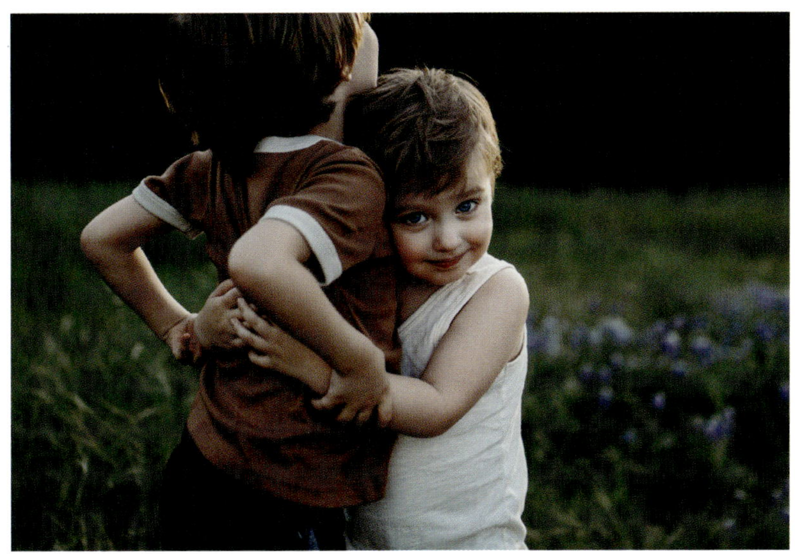

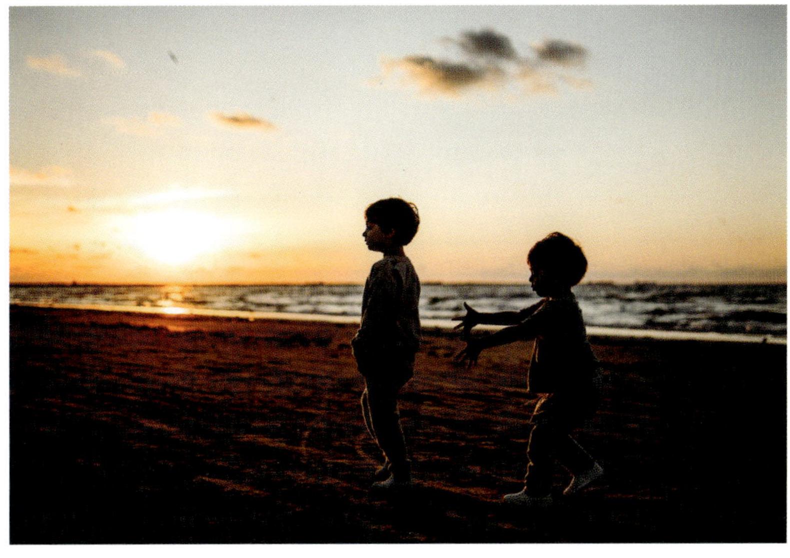

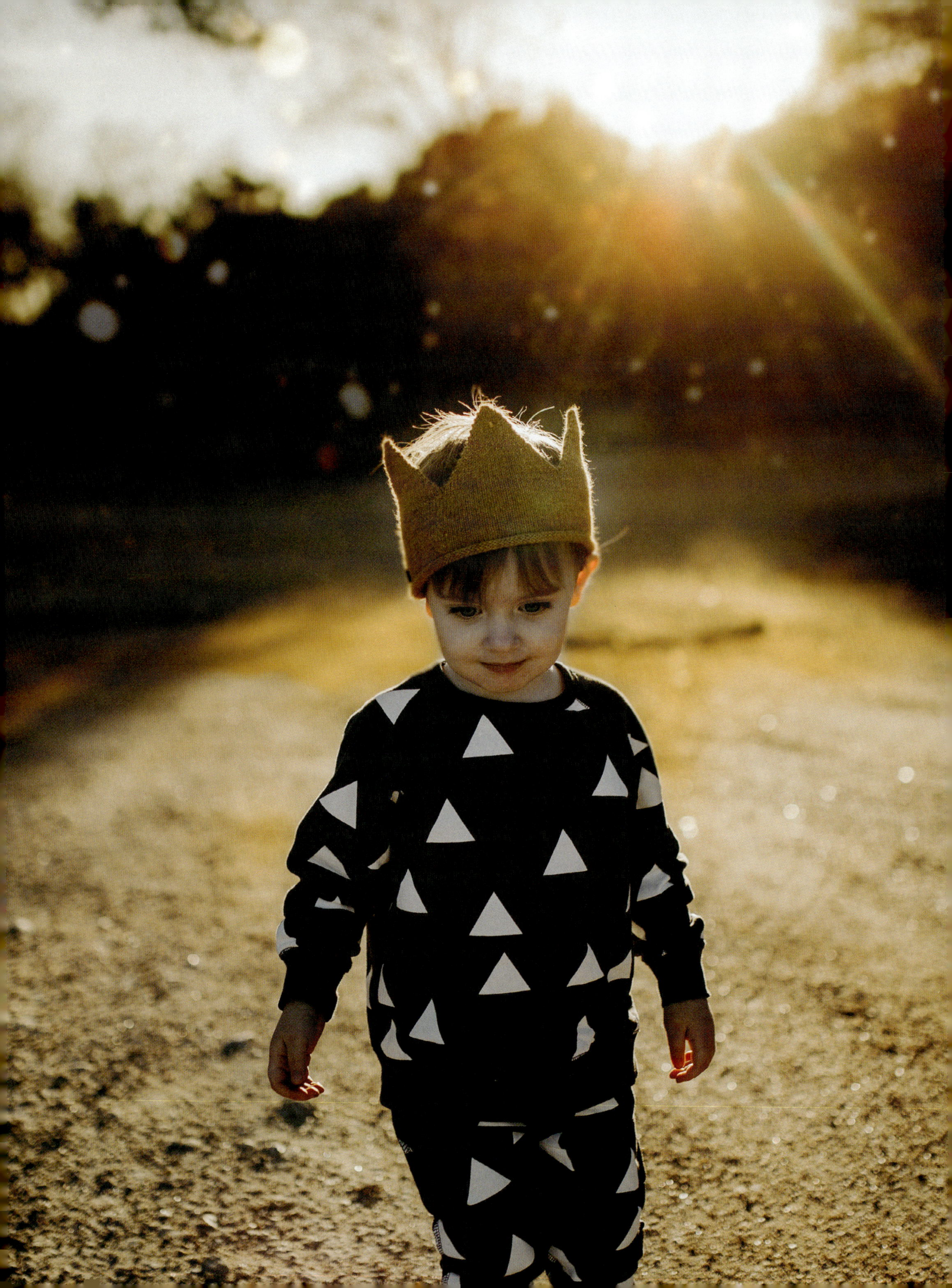

Autism, Again?

As Jude grew up, we started worrying about the possibility of him being autistic, too. At 16 months old, I still wasn't able to answer "yes" to any of those damn important questions. Pointing? Answering to his name? Talking? No, no, and hell no. I had to resist falling into a blind panic while filling out those questionnaires. But history was repeating itself. Just like Charlie, Jude didn't play with toys appropriately, he didn't talk, he flapped his hands, and he had sensory issues even more severe than Charlie's. Compared to the general population, the risk of autism is greater in siblings of people with autism, especially in boys, but there was nothing we could do about it except monitor Jude closely to get him the help he would need early.

We decided to get ahead of the game and got a referral with the developmental pediatrician that had diagnosed Charlie. Despite the fact that Jude failed the M-CHAT and scored in the 1st percentile for expressive and receptive speech, Dr. Jones was optimistic that Jude's symptoms could be due to other developmental delays that may correct themselves with therapies. Unlike his big brother, Jude had great joint-attention, the lack of which is a primary symptom of autism, and interacted well with his surroundings during his evaluation. Dr. Jones emphasized the need for Jude to be around neurotypical peers to learn. Up to that point, the only peer Jude had been around was Charlie. She suggested that we look for a school so Jude could be around children his own age and also recommended that we start speech therapy, occupational therapy, and physical therapy.

We chose a Montessori school that Jude started attending three days per week. I love that they teach children independence through play to give them confidence and teach them key skills. The learning is individualized for each child's unique needs and interests, and they also let children explore indoors and outdoors in a safe and respectful environment. These principles reminded me a lot of how I grew up in France, exploring my surroundings with a lot of freedom. I thought Jude may react well to it but most importantly, I knew how necessary it was for him to be around other kids who talk, sing, and socialize.

Within a few months of going to school and attending therapy, Jude's language skills exploded. He went from being completely nonverbal to being a chatterbox and a role model in his classroom. It was amazing to witness Jude's progression. And because we raised Charlie before we raised Jude, we learned not to take any milestone for granted. These milestones were incredible for us. When Jude started speaking and calling me "mommy," it was as if I had won the lottery—I was so relieved that he might not be autistic. I had finally earned the title I'd been wanting for so long: mommy.

At his 2-year checkup, I filled out that infamous questionnaire again. Pointing? Answering to his name? Talking? The joy I felt in that moment flooded my entire being, and with teary eyes and the biggest smile, I answered: yes, yes, and hell yes!

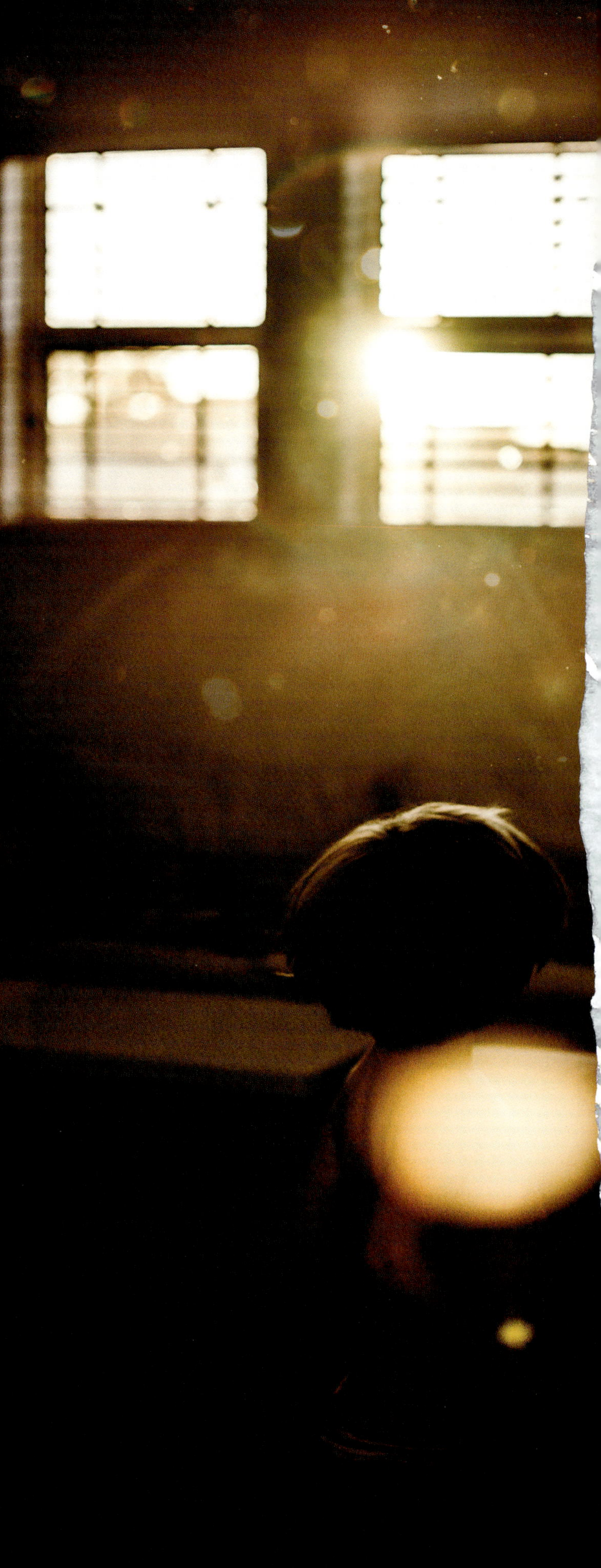

Crashing
the Party

Part of the pain autism brings has to do with fear. Fear about the uncertainty of Charlie's future and whether he will ever be able to learn self-care skills and find a way to communicate. But above all, there is a constant fear that Charlie will put himself in danger one too many times. There's the running in front of cars, his attraction to bodies of water despite his inability to swim, and the wandering away. That last one is very common among autistic children and a huge stressor on many families, including ours.

A few years back, I lived one of the scariest moments of my life. I still wonder what would have happened if Jude hadn't been here that day. It was a Sunday, and I was home alone with Charlie and Jude. The boys were watching TV in the living room and I was in the bathroom when Jude, who had limited speech back then, came running to me screaming, "Charlie! Charlie!" over and over again. There was a panicked tone to his voice. He was flapping his hands and looked totally shocked! I knew instantly that something was wrong and took off with Jude towards the living room. That's when I saw it: the front door, wide open. Charlie was gone. I was terrified.

I got an instant burst of adrenaline and my first reaction was to pick Jude up and run to the main street next to our house, a street known for cars driving too fast. Charlie wasn't there and I felt a sigh of relief that at least he wasn't lying injured in the road there. Our neighbor, who was outside, joined the search, and we took off in the other direction, shouting Charlie's name, even though I knew he wouldn't respond. It must have been ten excruciating minutes later, which felt like hours, when we found him. Two doors down from us began a little alleyway that curved around behind the houses. When I found Charlie at the end of it, he wasn't happy to see me. He was having fun, playing with rocks behind a pickup truck and had no idea he had done something bad. I had just crashed his party. He was mad at me for finding him and started screaming as I tried to direct him back home with a chubby baby Jude still in my arms.

I felt guilty for a while after that event because we knew Charlie could open doors and locks. He had not tried to escape in over a year so I let my guard down.

There was, however, a huge positive from this ordeal. Jude. He used to imitate Charlie all the time. In fact, he imitated so many of Charlie's behaviors that we thought he might be autistic, too. But not on that day. He was barely two then, but instead of following his big brother on an adventure in the streets, he alerted me. He knew it was wrong and I'd never been so proud of him. He very well may have saved Charlie's life!

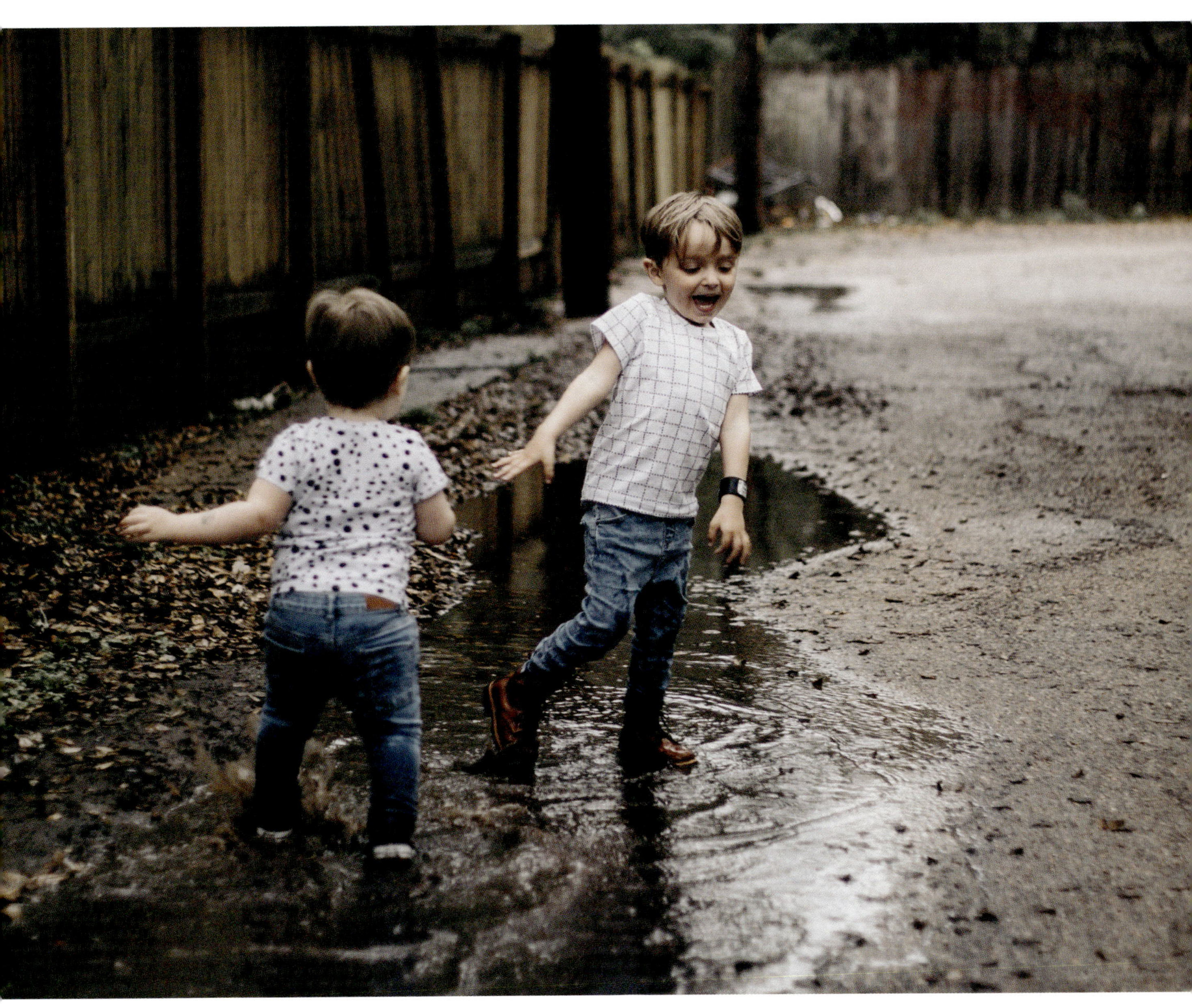

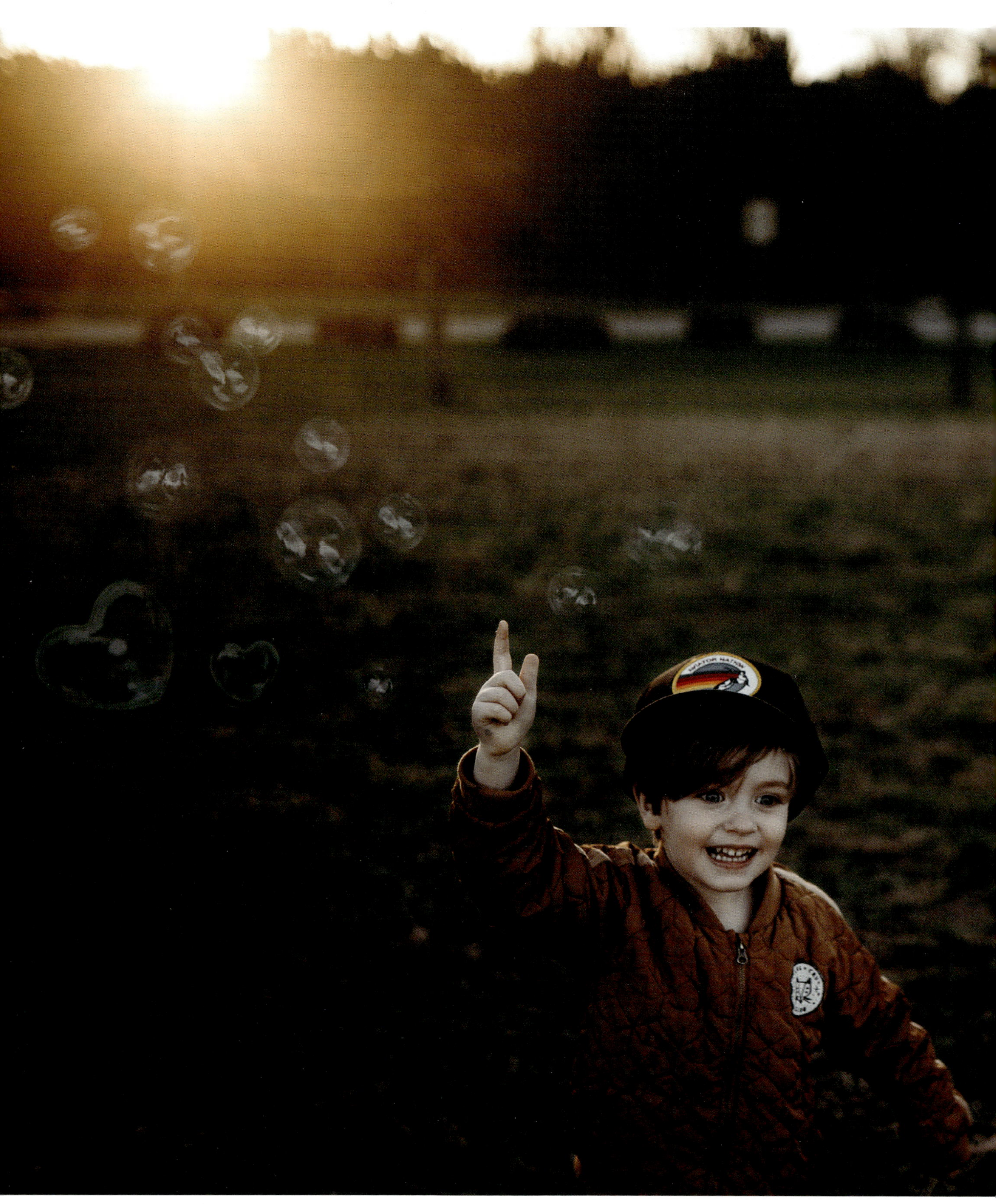

Wonder Child

I remember the joy I felt when Jude started talking. I felt so incredibly lucky, like I had just won the lottery. I'd hoped so intensely and for so long to have a child who could talk to me that it was overwhelming to finally have my wish come true. Jude started speaking around his second birthday, and he's been unstoppable since then. There's something so amazingly sweet about being able to have a conversation with the little human who grew inside of you. It doesn't mean that I love Charlie less because he can't communicate, but it makes my ability to have a discussion with Jude even more meaningful. I know communication is not a given, and I'm thankful every day for the gift of having a child who can communicate.

After Charlie started regressing, I always said that I'd give anything to have a child who calls me "mommy" 200 times a day. With Jude, I definitely got what I asked for. I've never seen a child as talkative as him. He never stops! Hell, he even talks to us in his sleep! He's constantly commenting on the world around him and asking questions about every little thing. In fact, so much so that I'm close to becoming that mom who complains on social media about her child talking too much! Okay, maybe not exactly that, but if I hadn't raised Charlie before Jude came around, I might have.

There are so many great moments that come with Jude learning to talk, like the way he mispronounces words such as "lasagna." And there's also something special about the way he tries to act like an adult. Jude has an amazing memory. He absorbs all the information he can and mimics everyone around him but doesn't necessarily have a good understanding of what he's learning, so it makes for some funny situations. He reminds me a lot of myself.

Last weekend, Willy and I were playing blocks with Jude when he turned to Willy and asked, "Hey, daddy, what time is it?" When Willy answered, "10:30," Jude paused for a second, put his hand pensively on his chin, and finally said, "Mmm, I don't know what that means." He's also told us that he wants to be a writer so he can drink wine and eat cake on the couch like mommy.

I hope he never loses his sense of wonder and desire to learn about everything. For now, I'm soaking in these memories and precious moments of him learning to talk and trying to make sense of the world around him.

I love you, too, Jude.

Now that Jude is 3, he's been asking a lot of questions about Charlie. Mommy, why Charlie doesn't want to play with me? Why Charlie can't talk? Why Charlie has autism?

I don't know that I've found a good answer to his questions yet. What does autism even mean to a 3-year-old? Probably not much. I've explained to Jude that Charlie has different abilities and needs than other kids and that he does love him even though he doesn't say it. That seemed to make sense to him, at least a little.

I've seen Jude say, "I love you" to Charlie, and after being met by silence, whisper to himself, "I love you, too, Jude," pretending the words came from Charlie.

Jude is such a sensitive boy. He loves Charlie unconditionally. No matter how many times Charlie pushes him away, Jude always forgives him. *It's okay, Charlie has autism. That's why he doesn't want a hug.* He helps Charlie in any way he can and takes care of him without expecting anything in return. He helps him brush his teeth, feed himself, use the bathroom, clean his face, and he even covers his ears to protect him from loud sounds. He gives so selflessly, and it amazes me.

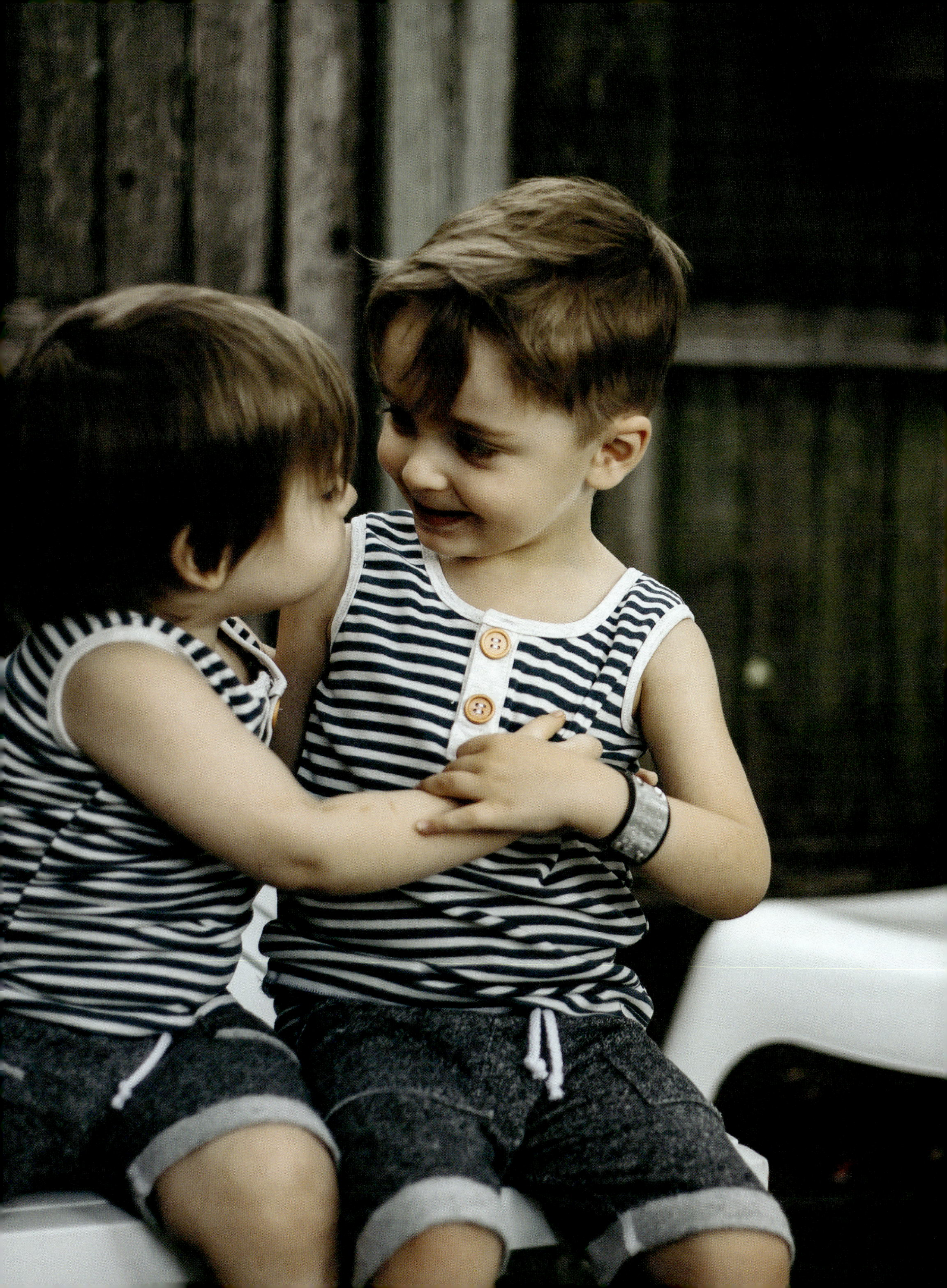

In the rare moments when Charlie gives back, Jude always smiles so widely. One particular time I remember he came running to me with tears in his eyes screaming, "Mommy! Charlie said 'hi' to me!" The pride and happiness he feels when Charlie overcomes a challenge or communicates with us in the simplest ways, we all feel in our family. It connects us. I know I feel it through my entire body. It's warm, and it fills my heart with hope and gratefulness.

When Charlie allows Jude to hug him, it makes me happy because these moments definitely are not a given in our household. I'm inspired by Jude and his big heart. I don't know many people who love like he does. He really gives it his all, and without fear, even though he's met with rejection more often than not.

On the flip side, I can't help but worry that being so soft will make Jude vulnerable as he gets older because we live in a world that shames sensitive boys. The expectation is that boys have to be strong. I wish for people to realize that feeling deeply has nothing to do with not being strong. Feeling deeply in a world where vulnerability is considered a sign of weakness shows strength. It takes courage to be your-self, to allow yourself whatever it is you need to feel in that moment. Of course, Jude doesn't have that level of thought yet. He feels deeply because that's who he is and he doesn't have the protective reaction from these emotions yet. But instead of encouraging him to not get so overwhelmed by his strong emotions, I encourage him to focus on his feelings and express them. I don't want Jude to "toughen up" and bottle up all his emotions. I did that for too long because this is what I was taught as a child. I don't want Jude to harden because the world expects him to. I do hope people will treat his fragile heart with kindness. All the love he gives so selflessly, he deserves to come back at him like a boomerang.

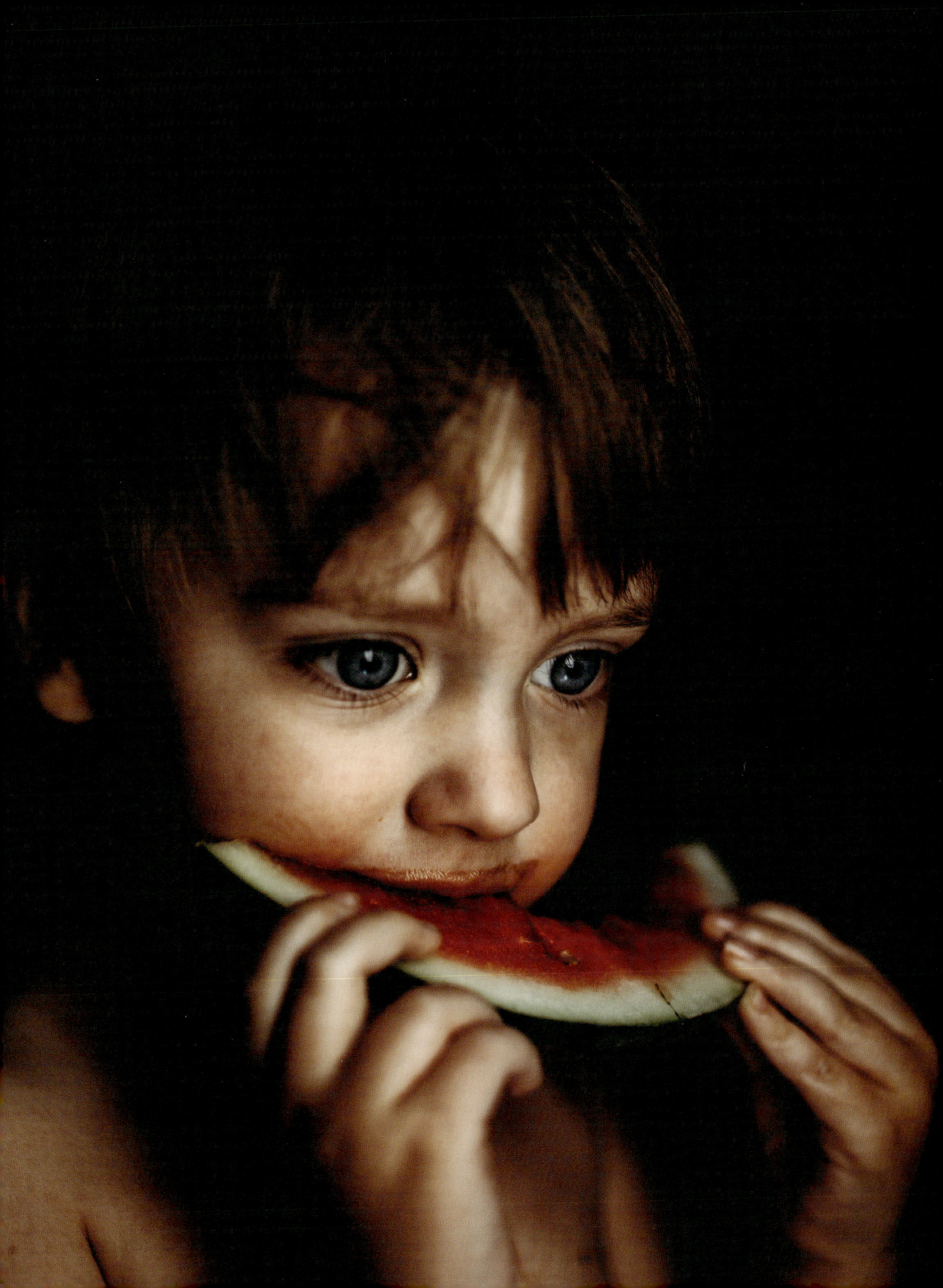

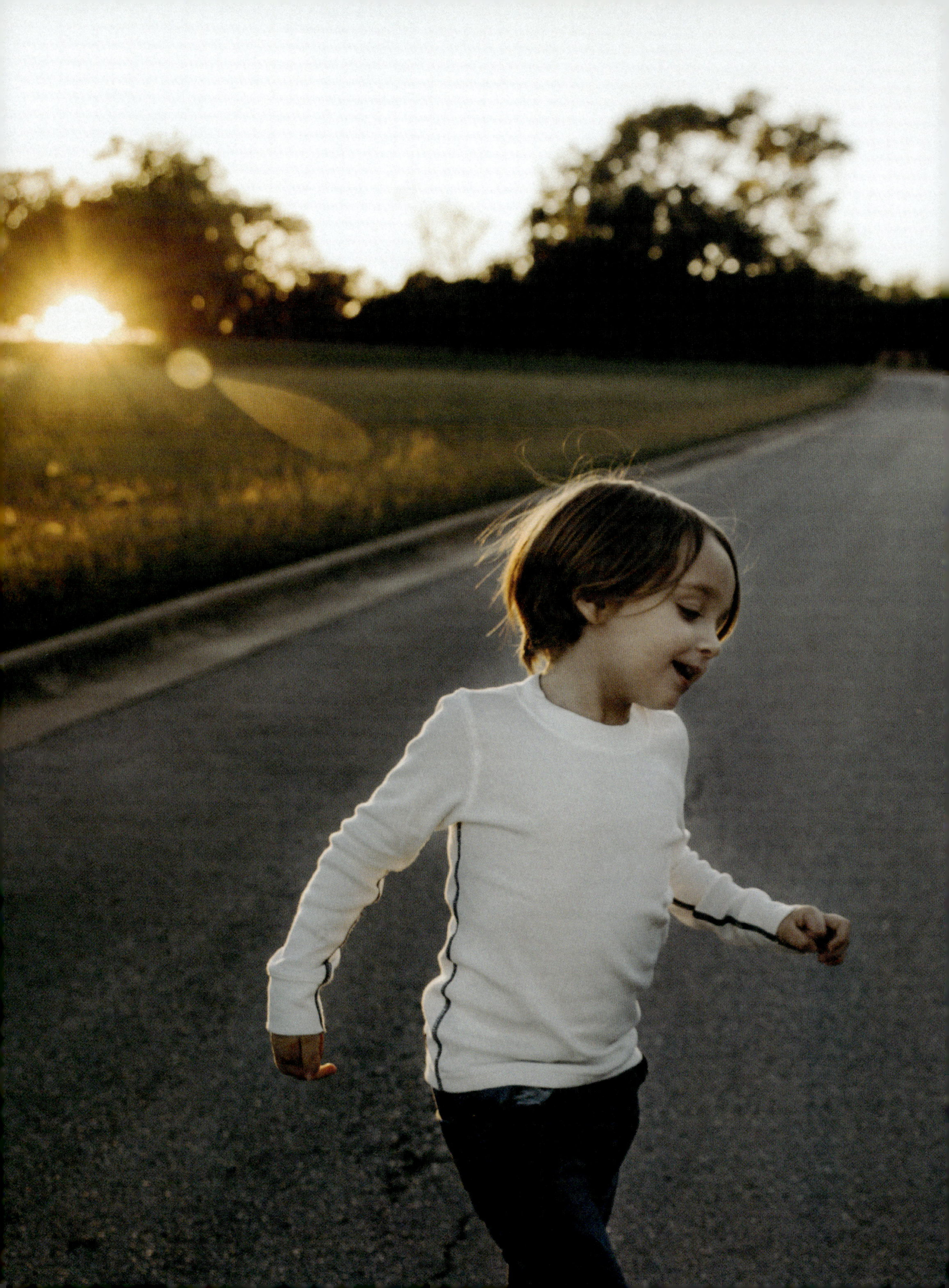

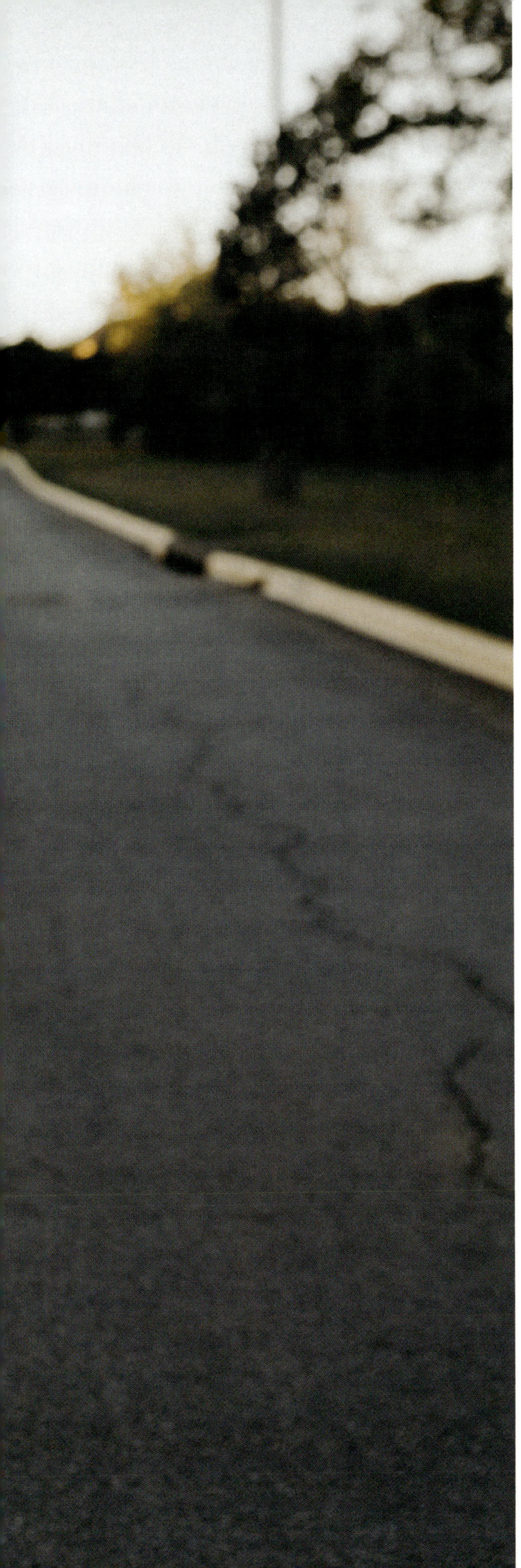

ABA Therapy

Just like society at large, the autism community is not unified in their beliefs about autism. The first time I mentioned ABA (Applied Behavior Analysis) therapy on my blog, it only took a few minutes before someone said to me, "You're torturing your child with ABA therapy." This didn't come as a surprise. Before Charlie was even diagnosed with autism I had searched the web for therapy options and found that ABA wasn't liked by everyone.

ABA is the number-one therapy recommended by medical experts for children on the autism spectrum; however, many autistics reject that conclusion.

As an autistic adult, I see both sides of the argument, but overall I'm in favor of ABA therapy.

I think a bit of context is necessary here. ABA therapy has evolved tremendously over the years. It's not the same as it was 60 years ago when Dr. O. Ivar Lovaas designed the first implementations of ABA to help autistic people.

He did so based on principles developed by famed psychologist B.F. Skinner, found in his book, published in 1938, *The Behavior of Organisms*. Back then they used robotic repetition of learning trials held in sterile rooms and administered punishment to help autistic people learn new and appropriate skills. In early behaviorism, rewards and punishments were used equally. Later, it became clear that rewards worked better than punishment, and punishment, while it might have encouraged learning for some, also produced fear. The methods used

ABA is not "one size fits all," and a good BCBA (Board Certified Behavior Analyst) will work hard to develop the best program for a child. For instance, we wanted Charlie to gain more independence, so our BCBA designed a program to teach him to brush his teeth and another one to teach him to put on his clothes by himself. There is no punishment if he can't do it, but if he does, he gets whatever reward he's into at the time. Some weeks that might be his tablet. Other weeks it might be a teaspoon of Nutella or a cookie.

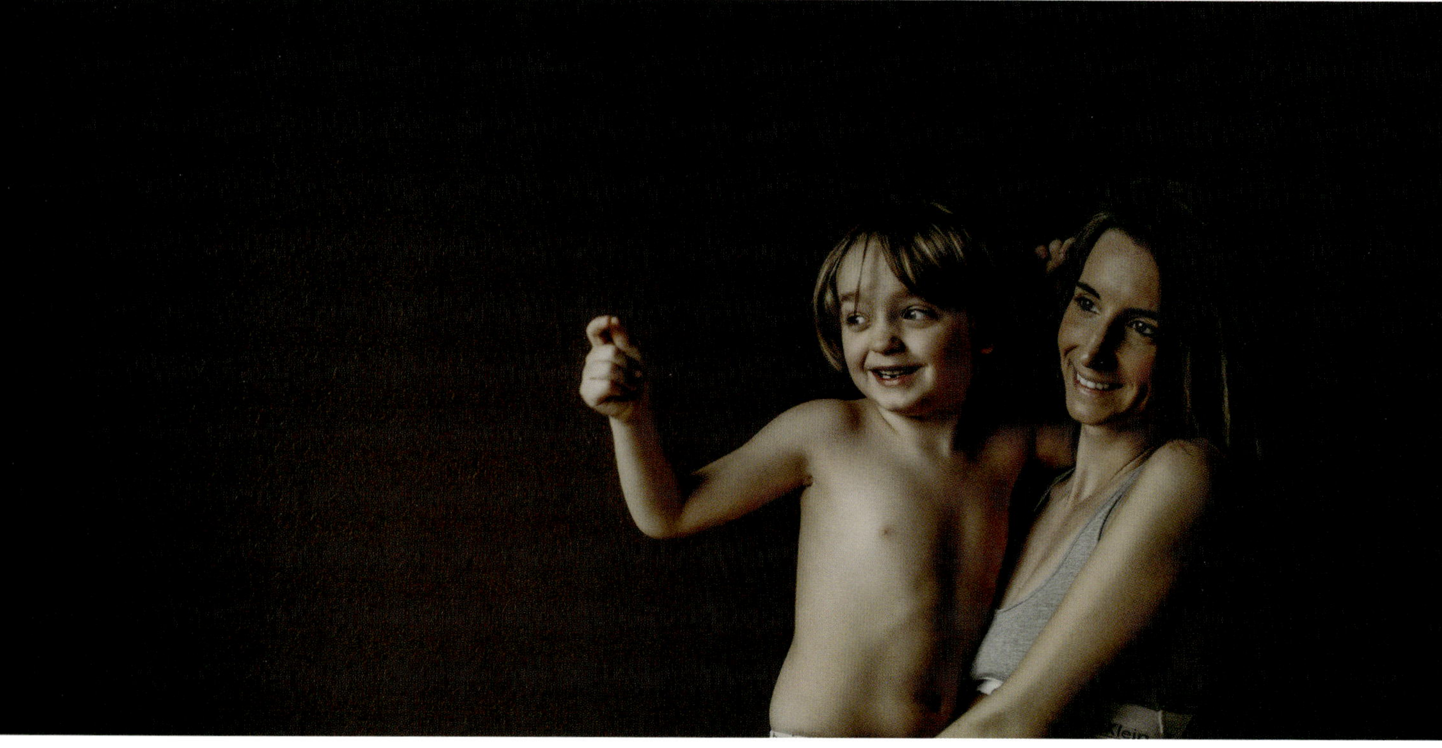

to help people with autism today have changed so much since Lovaas's initial experiments—it's unfair that they even bear the same name.

Charlie's ABA therapy is play-based. There are no punishments. Therapists may give a consequence to Charlie by taking a toy away from him if he's hitting them or screaming, but most parents do that with their children whether they're autistic or not.

The biggest criticism about ABA therapy is ableism, discrimination in favor of able-bodied people. I don't agree that ABA therapy is ableist. You can help someone without changing who they are. Charlie isn't in ABA therapy because we want him to be normal. We want him to be safe, independent, and to learn to communicate, to decrease his, and yes, our frustration. We want to fade away the less functional and dangerous behaviors, like playing with the cats' litter box, swallowing rocks, and running in the street, to give him a better shot at life. I'm not trying to "fix" Charlie's autism. Therapy is here to make his life easier by providing him with ways to communicate, and most importantly keeping him safe. If it takes giving him a cookie to make him stop these dangerous behaviors and learn self-care, as well as communication, then I'm okay with it.

Everyone working with Charlie is amazing. But not all BCBAs, therapists, and therapy centers are great. Some of them are poorly run and the methods used are imprecise and borderline abusive. Though this is becoming less common, it may explain the more current ABA horror stories you read on the internet. It's important that parents choose an ABA center that aligns with their values, a place where therapists and BCBAs will listen to them when they have concerns or don't feel comfortable with the way a specific skill is being taught.

On the flip side, there is a part of me that sees how ABA can sometimes be harmful to autistic people. For instance, some ABA therapists may prevent a child from flapping his hands or rocking. To me, there's nothing wrong with stimming (self-stimulating behavior) as long as it doesn't get in the way of learning. In school, hopefully, the teachers will teach the other children what it means, rather than try to get Charlie to stop because the other children don't understand it. But I also get it: Constant stimming may prevent a child from focusing in class. I don't think we, autistic people, should have to change to fit in with neurotypical people, but I also want Charlie to have all the opportunity he can possibly have to learn, and maybe that does mean preventing him from stimming in certain situations. The balance, between wanting people to accept the

non-harmful behaviors autistics often engage in and wanting Charlie to be accepted and able to focus in real-life situations, is sometimes difficult to find.

ABA therapy has been a huge help for Charlie and for us. It saddens me how little importance is given to parents of autistic children. I get that sickening feeling in my stomach when people tell me that I'm torturing Charlie with ABA and that Charlie learning to communicate and developing self-care skills isn't important because what matters is that he's happy. Charlie is perfectly happy playing in the cat's litter box. Charlie's happy banging his head on the wall. Charlie's happy running in the street in front of cars. How about Charlie's safety? How about me as a mother? Should I let my child put himself in danger because he's happy? Charlie isn't happy either when he can't communicate and make himself heard. Thanks to his ABA therapists, Charlie can now communicate basic needs with an app on his iPad called ProloQuo2go.

I was at a loss before ABA therapy came into our life. There's no way I could have accomplished what Charlie's therapists did for him on my own. An autistic child grows up in a world comprised almost completely of neurotypical people, and they have to learn how to function within it. ABA's ultimate goal is to help autistic people live an independent, safe, and happy life in this world—and I think that's wonderful. While I understand some of the concerns with ABA therapy, in my opinion, when done well, administered by caring people who are open to criticism and who keep a child's best interest in mind, ABA is the best therapy for children on the autism spectrum.

The Puzzle Piece Symbol?

The origins of the puzzle piece as a symbol for autism go back to 1963. It was created by Gerald Gasson, a parent and board member for the National Autistic Society (formerly The Society for Autistic Children) in London, England. Back then, they believed autistic people suffered from a "puzzling" condition.

Puzzle piece protesters believe that the puzzle piece implies that there is a mystery to be solved. I personally don't find this to be hurtful.

Autism is a mysterious, puzzling condition. We don't know the causes, and that's what makes us unique.

I also think it's a good symbol to represent the difference between each autistic individual, who, just like puzzle pieces, each has our own way of fitting in.

Some autistics worry that the symbolism behind it indicates that people on the autism spectrum are "missing" a piece. That's one way to see it, but to me, it's not so much a missing piece but more of a necessary piece, the one that makes us who we are. It's all about perspective and interpretation.

Some autistics despise the puzzle piece logo because it's used by Autism Speaks. Many believe that this autism organization speaks on behalf of autistic people without their best interests in mind. They believe that as the organization doesn't include autistic board members it cannot truly speak for people with autism and in fact, they're just profiting off our disability. Personally, I don't have anything against Autism Speaks, but perhaps my expectations for an autism organization are low because I grew up in a country with zero autism awareness. To me, if people are talking about autism openly and respectfully, then it's great. If there had been more widespread awareness of autism while I was growing up in France in the 90s, I probably would not have spent so many years as an adult trying to figure out what was "wrong" with me.

Vaccines and Autism?

When I became a mom, I quickly realized that I was going to have to make choices. A lot of choices. Sometimes hard choices. Circumcision or not? Breastfeeding or formula? Co-sleeping or no? Baby-wearing or stroller? Some of these decisions are simply a parenting style choice, but there are some choices that can have lasting and important consequences. Vaccination is one of these. As an autistic mother of an autistic child, I often get asked: Do you vaccinate? Do you believe vaccines cause autism?

In 1998, a doctor named Andrew Wakefield published a study with falsified evidence claiming that he found a link between the MMR (Measles-Mumps-Rubella) vaccine and autism. The study was tiny, with only 12 people sampled. The paper was eventually retracted and Wakefield lost his license to practice medicine. Unfortunately, the idea that these shots cause autism stuck in people's minds. Since then, there have been more than 20 in-depth studies done on the MMR vaccine and autism that show no link between the two.

Meanwhile, outbreaks of measles and whooping cough continue to appear in the United States and Europe, putting thousands of kids at risk of death, almost entirely as the result of parents refusing to vaccinate their children because of anecdotal horror stories heard from people against immunization.

I vaccinated Charlie. Yes, he's severely autistic, but there's no scientific evidence that vaccines cause autism. The fact that autism symptoms appear after the MMR shot is a coincidence of timing. Early autism signs are most recognizable after about 18 months of age, which happens to coincide with the recommended timing for the MMR vaccine. For Charlie, the signs of autism were there before the vaccines anyway. Jude is fully on track with his vaccination schedule, too. No regrets!

And what if vaccines did cause autism? Well, I'm autistic and I have a severely autistic child, and I'm happy to be alive. Sure it's not always easy for him—and for me—to live with autism but we are healthy and alive! Polio, whooping cough, and other diseases that vaccines protect against are miserable and potentially deadly. People don't know the nightmarish realities of these diseases because due to vaccines, we've been protected from them for years. To my surprise, most autistic adults seem to share my views on vaccines. Or should I say "adults with autism"? Yet another controversy dividing people.

Person-First Language

Some people feel strongly about calling themselves Autistic with a capital A. Others like to be referred to as a "person with autism." Still others like to say they're on the autism spectrum. I don't care about the terminology at all, as long as people are respectful, but I usually describe myself as being autistic or being an Aspie, and sometimes as having autism. To me, this is a non-issue. People can call me whatever they'd like, as long as it's respectful.

On the other end, many autistics prefer to be called autistic because they believe that autism is not an add-on to their personality but something foundational to their identity. To them, it's the same concept as referring to a person of the Jewish faith as Jewish as opposed to a person with Jewishness. We get that it's not the only identity the person has, but it's still foundational. The term "with autism" makes it sound like the autism can be taken away from the person, when that is not true. It's impossible to detach autism from an autistic person.

Obviously, my nonchalant attitude towards this issue has led to some hate, yet again, from members of the #ActuallyAutistic community. One of them told me that I couldn't possibly be autistic or else I wouldn't call myself a person with autism but an autistic person. I was taken aback by the absurdity of his comment. I'm still unsure how that makes sense, but he seemed very sure of himself!

A Cure for Autism?

There's this other big question that divides the autism community: Should we try to find a cure for autism? Autism impacts people's lives on different levels. Some individuals, like Charlie, are severely disabled, while others, like me, are able to live an independent life. I'm not surprised that people at both ends of the spectrum would have different opinions on this issue.

It upsets me when I read articles written by parents titled, "How I cured my child's autism." Just this morning, I stumbled upon a news article promoting an episode of a famous French documentary-style show that has been airing nationally every Sunday for 18 years, similar to *60 Minutes* in the United States. The story was about a mother who claimed to have cured her daughter's autism. She described her now teenage daughter as a completely "normal" and successful adult. The comments section made me angry because most people were inspired by the story, congratulating the mom for working so hard to cure her child.

I wish people understood that autism is not a disease. Autism is a disability and you can't cure it. Symptoms can improve but you are born autistic and will always be. These inspirational stories exist for two possible reasons:

The child was never autistic to begin with and received an inaccurate diagnosis, or the symptoms of autism have simply improved and the child has learned to "pass" so well that the disability isn't visible anymore. These types of stories from parents really bother me because I feel like they're not portraying autism as it really is. The fact that they think autism is curable demonstrates a lack of understanding.

Hypothetically, what if there were a cure? What if there were a way to improve our symptoms?

I think we can all agree that the ability to communicate is important and so are the abilities to eat without gagging, being able to use the bathroom by ourselves, staying safe, and making friends. Then shouldn't we be able to agree that if there were a way to provide autistic individuals with these skills, it would be beneficial?

If there were a cure, I would take it myself. I'm high-functioning, but autism affects me in ways that hinder my own happiness and sometimes those around me, too. I want to be able to make friends. I want to be able to go to the store by myself without feeling the need to take two days off afterward. I want to be able to enjoy social gatherings and fireworks. I want the ability to not obsess over things I don't have control over. I want to be able to look at people in the eyes so I can connect with them. For all of these reasons and more, if there were a cure I'd take it.

How about Charlie and other severely affected individuals who can't make that decision for themselves, though? That's where it gets tricky. As his mom, should I be able to make that decision for Charlie? What negative consequences could come from curing his autism? Fortunately, since there aren't any cures for autism, I don't have to make a decision yet.

When I think about all the controversies in the autism world, what strikes me is the lack of respect people have for one another on both sides of the fence. We all need to learn to have some tolerance for differing views. I do see some benefits to my own high-functioning autism, but overall it impacts my life more negatively than positively. Some people on the severe end of the spectrum see no benefit at all to autism, while other high-functioning individuals are so proud of being autistic that they became advocates to show the rest of the world how awesome autism is. Whatever it is that we feel, we all deserve to be respected for our opinions.

———————————————————————

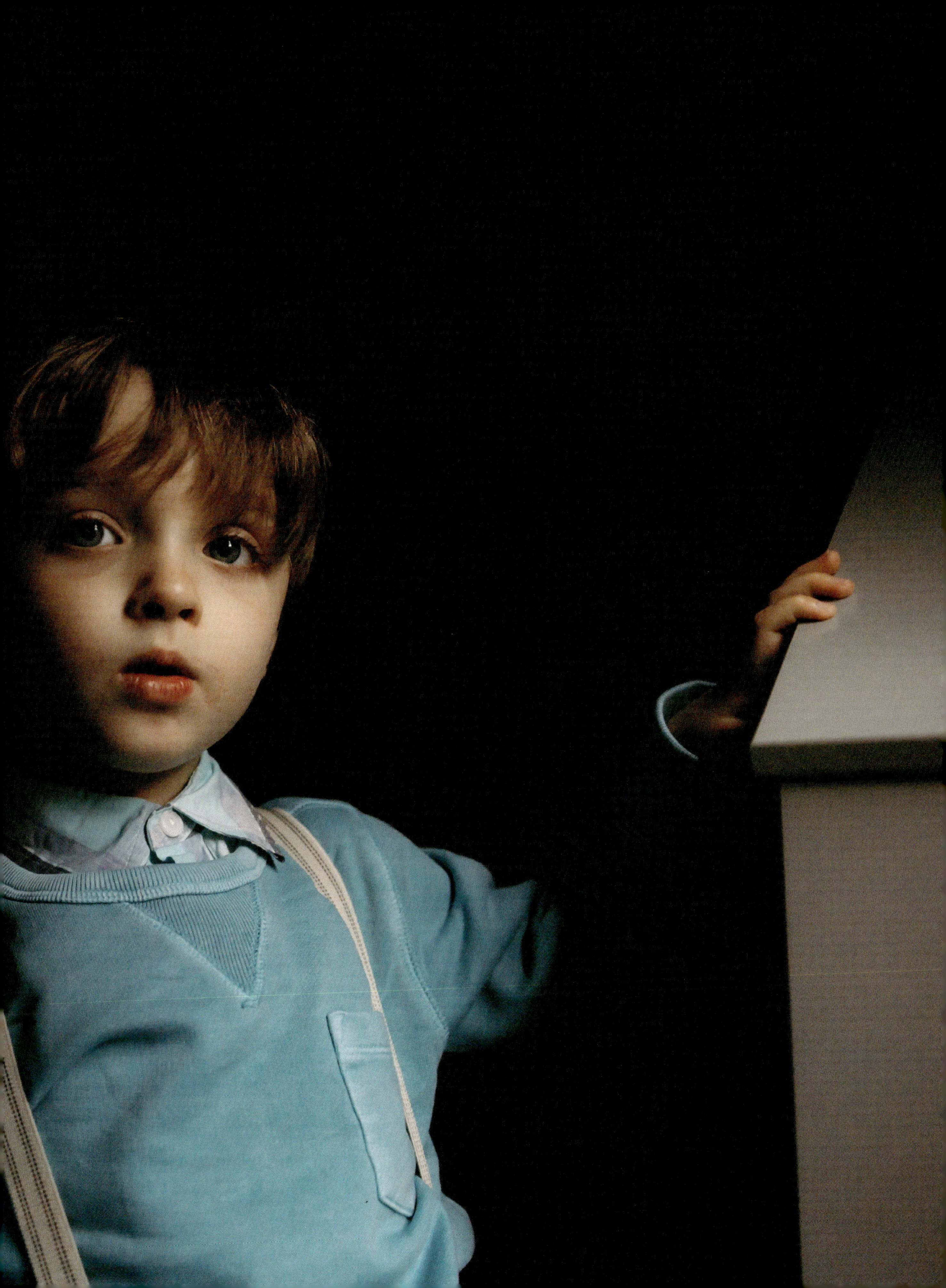

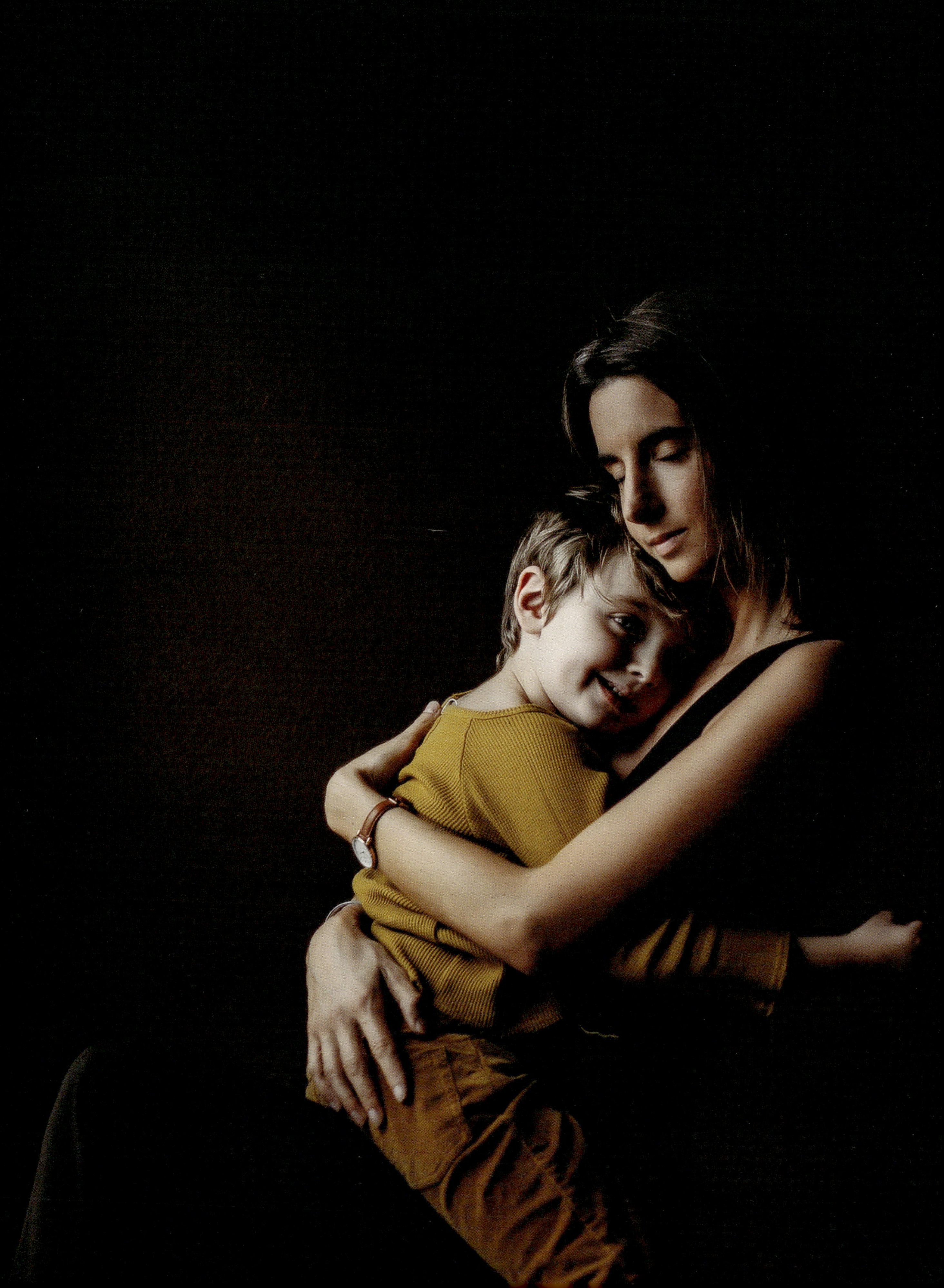

Growing up with an undiagnosed disability in a country that lacks acceptance for people who are different was difficult, but I've learned from it. My hometown, Troyes, is beautiful. It's the medieval village in which Chretien de Troyes, the 12th-century poet, wrote the Arthurian legend and probably even created the characters of Lancelot and Percival who searched for the Holy Grail. Downtown, half-timbered houses, straight out of history books and fairytales, line the streets. As a child, I was in awe every time I walked past them. There are beautiful gardens, little boutiques, and streets with friendly wild cats and people drinking in a café *en terrasse* on the streets.

As the years went by, I stopped noticing it all. Like with many young people, I didn't see the beauty of my hometown anymore, as if my senses had been broken down. I only had one goal; making it from point-A to point-B without being accosted by a stranger. The anxiety I experienced walking these streets shaped me. It had me constantly looking over my shoulder, on high alert, searching for a signal that everything would be okay. My eyes had stared at those same cobbled streets for so long that I knew where I was simply by looking at the specific stones in the road. I didn't even need to look up to get home. I knew these streets like the back of my hand.

I became scared of strangers' possible reactions. What were they going to say to me today? What did they see when they looked at me? I'd have rather bumped my head walking into a post than look at people. I couldn't make eye contact or they would have seen right through me, seen a wholly insecure girl who was deeply broken on the inside. I was an easy target. I couldn't take that risk.

Over the years, I've put myself out there and I've taken risks, admittedly with little success. I've invested in relationships, I've kept my head up walking in the street, and I've stayed soft after having been hurt over and over again. I've stumbled more times than I can remember, but I try not to regret any of it. All the pain I felt after each failure, each betrayal, that pain made me grow into the person I am today. There was never a losing moment even if it felt that way at first because eventually there was always a valuable lesson to be learned. I've been beaten up, made fun of, rejected, betrayed, and spat on…and not only have I survived, but I've also grown from it.

Troyes and My Holy Grail

Thinking of my compatriot Chretien de Troyes and his characters who searched for the Holy Grail, I wonder what the Holy Grail of autism might be. I wouldn't presume to say that we need to find a cure for autism, as I do see that many autistic adults do quite well with it, and even thrive. For some people, it becomes a positive part of their identity they truly value.

What I do hope is that autism therapies advance and become more readily available so that everyone with autism is able to fully communicate and take care of themselves. I want my home country, as well as my new country, to see how important it is to financially support therapy for autistic children, to emotionally support the parents of autistic children, and to fill schools with the much-needed trained individuals who can help our children to advance and learn. And I want people to be kinder and more tolerant when they meet someone whose brain is wired differently than theirs.

My personal Holy Grail? What I yearn for most is for Charlie to be able to keep himself safe, to be able to talk and express himself, to learn self-care and hygiene, to be happy, and dare I say call me "mommy," all while still being himself.

And I yearn for a friend to travel this lonely road with me. Someone with whom I can be honest and who will be honest back. Someone who will break down my walls and still stay after seeing the scars. Someone to drink rosé with on the roof of a building. Someone who'll give me tough love when I'm off the mark. Someone who will see the pain behind my smile and reassure me that everything is going to be okay. Someone who will love me when I feel unlovable. Someone to laugh with me until our faces hurt. And someone who will hug me instead of judging me if I'm crying because on that day autism is too much.

In a world that can be harsh, I wish for everyone to find a person who will make them feel like they're not alone. We are not alone. We just need to find our people. ∎

10 Tips for After Your Child Gets

1. Therapy

There's really no shame in getting your child or yourself into therapy. Getting an official diagnosis will allow your child to qualify for all kinds of therapy (speech therapy, occupational therapy, DIR therapy, and ABA therapy). Do some research, call around, and find what therapy looks best for your child. We do ABA therapy and speech therapy. Don't hesitate to shop around to find the therapy center that best fits your child's needs. It's a big decision, so don't be afraid to be picky and to advocate with school systems and health insurance companies.

2. Routine

A fixed schedule is important for a child on the autism spectrum. Most autistic children/adults do not like when their routine is disrupted. They like to know what's coming. Transitions are hard, too, so use a timer if you have to change activity. Tell your child, "okay, in one minute we're going to go back inside." All the therapists use this trick and we have incorporated it at home. It may not work right away, but if you're consistent your child will understand the concept of a timer and it will decrease your and your child's frustration while transitioning from one activity to another.

3. Celebrate

Every milestone is worth celebrating, no matter how small! Your child may be delayed developmentally. I like to think of Charlie as developing on his own timeline. His milestones and successes may be different from his peers—different from what your friends are celebrating about their kids—but they're totally worth celebrating. Celebrate your child's victories even if they appear small. The first time Charlie said the sound "buh" for bubbles when he was three, we broke out the champagne.

4. One-on-one Time

Do whatever you can to spend quality time with your child. I know it can be difficult because they may not even want you to play with them, but do it anyway. Take him or her to the park. Don't stay home because it's easier. I made that mistake in the beginning. You have to confront the outside world even if it's overwhelming and scary for you both. It'll get easier. Let them explore like you would if you had a neurotypical child.

Diagnosed With Autism

5. Support

Autism can be isolating. I know this first-hand. It's important to find people you can talk to, people who are going through the same thing you are, and who "get it." Finding support groups online or in your local area is important. I should take my own advice, shouldn't I?

6. Don't Compare

Comparison is the thief of joy. This is hard because you see your friend's children doing the things you'd pictured yourself doing with your kiddo. They're celebrating different milestones but it doesn't mean you shouldn't celebrate yours (see #3).

7. Praise Your Child

Most kids on the autism spectrum understand and love positive reinforcement even if they don't always show it. Congratulate them! Make them feel proud of their accomplishments!

8. Take Care of Yourself

This is really important. I struggle with this myself, but in order to be able to care for your child, who may require extra attention, you need to feel good. Once in a while, leave the kiddos with a trusted caregiver or babysitter and do something you like. Whether it's hanging out with your friends, having a glass of wine, taking a walk, going to Target, or going to the gym, do something that makes *you* happy. You need it to function at your best.

9. Ignore Negative or Ignorant People

You will inevitably meet people who will say things like, "Oh, but he's so cute, are you sure he's autistic?" Or "Autism is just a new trend," or "He just needs a good spanking," or "Stop whining about your child's autism, you martyr mom!"

Don't let these comments get to you and stay focused on the positive. Focus on your child, focus on yourself, and focus on all the other people in your life who "get it" and support you in your journey. If you have the energy, educate others, but don't feel it's your obligation to do so.

10. Free Resources

There are many free resources and programs for children on the autism spectrum. In Texas, programs like DADS and DARS have long waiting lists, but they're worth it. There's also respite care, Early Childhood Intervention if your child is under three, and free preschool programs for children with disabilities. It will vary from state to state, so ask around. Ask your child's doctor.

Acknowledgments

I'd like to start by thanking my boys, Charlie and Jude. Thank you for loving me when I'm not the perfect mom, thank you for being the sweet and gentle souls that you both are in a world that can sometimes be harsh. I hope life treats you well and that people accept you for the amazing boys you are. Huge thanks also go to my husband, Willy. Thank you for entertaining the boys so I could write, thank you for hugging me when I doubted myself, and thank you for supporting me in spite of the time this book took away from us.

I would be remiss if I did not thank Lorin, my manager. Thank you for your invaluable help with this book. But even more, thank you for your kindness and for being in my life. I'm lucky to call you a friend. Thanks also to Shine Influencers, without whom this book wouldn't have been possible. Thank you for your support and your help with finding a publisher. And to that publisher, too, thank you. Thank you to the wonderful people at Thought Catalog who made this book come to life; there's no better home I could imagine for *All Across the Spectrum*. Thanks, Noelle, Bianca, and Kristina.

More thanks go to my *maman*, Kathleen Dumoulin. Thank you for your patience. I know it must have been difficult at times to raise a child like me. And also thank you for spreading autism awareness and acceptance in France, along with Tom. Thanks to my dad, Marc Geoffroy, for coming to visit us in Texas and showing Jude how to build castles. I would especially like to thank my mother-in-law, Sharon Lamb. Thank you for your support and help with this book. I'm grateful, too, to the people who provide Charlie with therapy every day, and to my own therapist, Dr. R., who's helped me through this process.

Finally, thank you to my followers online. I couldn't have done this without you. I hope you find comfort in this book and know that you are not alone in this journey. We are not alone.

Eileen Lamb ————————————

Eileen Lamb, founder of The Autism Cafe, is a writer and photographer. Born in France, she now lives in Austin, Texas, with her husband and two sons, Charlie and Jude. On her blog, she shares the ups and downs of raising a severely autistic child while being on the autism spectrum herself. In her free time, Eileen enjoys daydreaming, wine, and road trips.

instagram.com/theautismcafe
theautismcafe.com
facebook.com/theautismcafe

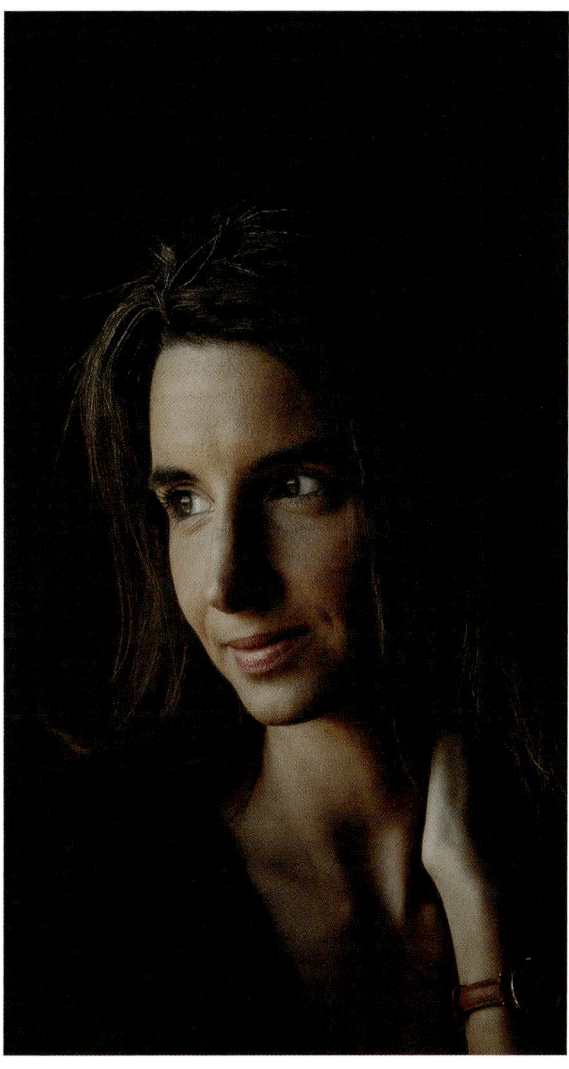

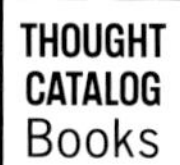

Published by Thought Catalog Books, an imprint of the digital magazine Thought Catalog which is owned and operated by The Thought & Expression Company LLC, an independent media organization based in Brooklyn, New York and Los Angeles, California. Printed in the United States of America.

ISBN 978-1-949759-10-5

This book was produced by Chris Lavergne and Noelle Beams. Art direction and design by KJ Parish. Special thanks to Bianca Sparacino for creative editorial direction and Isidoros Karamitopoulos for circulation management.

Visit us on the web at thoughtcatalog.com and shopcatalog.com.